HOMELESS
to
HOPKINS

My Journey From Homeless Teenager to
Becoming a Physician at the World-Renowned
Johns Hopkins Hospital

CHRISTOPHER L. SMITH, M.D.

MINDSTIR MEDIA

Published by Mindstir Media, LLC
45 Lafayette Rd | Suite 181| North Hampton, NH 03862 | USA
1.800.767.0531 | www.mindstirmedia.com

Printed in the United States of America

ISBN: 978-1-958729-50-2 (Paperback)
ISBN: 978-1-958729-51-9 (Hardback)

DEDICATION

I want to dedicate this book to all the precious souls out there going through what I went through. Don't lose hope and don't give up. I also want to acknowledge my wife Teena Smith, who has helped me through this journey. She has been an invaluable support in reading my memoir and offering suggestions. Without her in my life, this story would not have happened. She is the truly best part of my life.

A portion of all proceeds from book sales will be donated to charity.

CONTENTS

Foreword...vii

Chapter 1   Scars 1
Chapter 2   Early Childhood 5
Chapter 3   Later Childhood... 17
Chapter 4   Middle School and High School.........................33
Chapter 5   Becoming Homeless 39
Chapter 6   Homeless 43
Chapter 7   Alone..47
Chapter 8   Stumbling Forward 51
Chapter 9   Conflicting Journeys and, Of Course, Prom........53
Chapter 10   Dances..59
Chapter 11   High School Graduation 63
Chapter 12   Family Falling Apart..71
Chapter 13   Alone, Finding My Own Path 75
Chapter 14   College!..79
Chapter 15   Quitting and Beginning Again 83
Chapter 16   Mission: Missionary Work 87
Chapter 17   Life after a Mission.. 103
Chapter 18   Dating Life 111
Chapter 19   From Friendship to Relationship 121
Chapter 20   Wedding Day and "Wedding Receptions"........... 129
Chapter 21   Newlyweds 133
Chapter 22   Breaking Free.. 137
Chapter 23   Creating a New Life..145
Chapter 24   Growing Together..151
Chapter 25   Application and Acceptance...............................161
Chapter 26   Medical School Begins..169

Chapter 27 Adoption 175

Chapter 28 Residency Applications 191

Chapter 29 Match Day 195

Chapter 30 Moving On 199

Chapter 31 Haley 205

Chapter 32 Hopkins 211

Chapter 33 Desires and Outcomes 215

Chapter 34 Afterword 219

Epilogue 221

FOREWORD

We often find ourselves thinking that we are incapable or unable to achieve the goals we may have set for ourselves or the dreams that we may have contemplated in our lives. We have limited beliefs about what we can and cannot do based on our upbringing, our heritage and our surroundings. I watched my father try to become an author which is no small task given his father, Ernest Hemingway was one of the greatest writers of the 20th century, 21st century and likely many centuries to come. For me and my sisters and probably indeed for my father we wanted to achieve something of merit because it is how we have defined ourselves throughout our family history. In my case my genetics literally screamed out for me to accomplish some sort of creative viability to gain acknowledgement. I wanted be be noticed because of that genetic trait. Becoming an actress at a young age, I was able to find a way to express myself creatively that was rewarding enough to make me feel my existence. Being applauded publicly gave me a sense of purpose however unhealthy that might have been. For me it was an expression that was uniquely mine in my family that valued words written rather than spoken

But you have decided to read this book not because of what I have done in my life but as a way to explore how a man, Dr. Christopher Smith can become his full potential through the shadows and darkness he overcame. I mention my own life (and heritage) to bring context to the idea that our stories build our character and our character is a reflection of our experiences. How we achieve our success is unique to each individual. Dr. Smith's obstacles would normally have emotionally crippled another man. What I believe inspires you in reading this book and certainly why it fascinates me, is the human triumph that Chris expresses on every page. Plus he writes elegantly, with total transparency and honesty. I think we are all intrigued by those people that defy the world's limitations. And besides, aren't limitations purely set in place by upbringing, trauma or a culture that says, 'under these circumstances you can't become who you want to be...' or an inner voice that says we can only do so much in your life... Those blocks are made up and you have to confront them to defeat them.

Chris Smith's book is about those confrontations and how he achieves his dreams through difficult circumstances. The most challenging, his mental state. Anxiety and depression was a difficulty he fought against and overcame. Chris has dealt with so much. At a young age he survived a suicide attempt. And yet his instinctual courage to get past his wavering mind and become not just successful but inspiring is a triumph. What looks impossible to someone from the outside world is what drives him forward. Like me, I believe, you'll read this book in awe of Chris' strength of character. Dr. Smith has done more in this world than the world could have ever expected of him and even that he might have expected from himself. He has a drive to survive that demands you keep reading. He has moments of losing his way and even losing his faith in God. Whatever his trouble he always course corrects and guides himself back on task. A young person navigating homelessness and getting into medical school and eventually becoming a doctor is, in my opinion, mind blowing.

Against all odds is really the only way I can describe **Homeless To Hopkins**. When everything around him tells him to give up (even himself) he perseveres. This is, not only an American success story, it is a human expression of inner faith... from his personal belief that the only way up is through and when you push through the challenges there is actually peace. Chris' book is an inspiration for anyone asking themselves if they can do it (achieve their dreams) or if it's even possible. After reading this book I would say you will have your answer and that answer is *yes*, anything and everything is possible if you keep making the choice be more than you were yesterday.

Mariel Hemingway
Oscar and Emmy Nominated Actress, Best- Selling Author
and granddaughter of Ernest Hemingway

CHAPTER 1

Scars

Most of our lives we live in a trance, dealing with what's in front of us, going through the motions to get through, get around, get by: the daily time and motion of life. This is especially true for the punishing schedule of a resident physician at The Johns Hopkins Hospital, where you live on an electronic leash, the beeper lashed to your belt like a prisoner's ankle bracelet. Sometimes, though, something happens that takes you out of the trance and reminds you of what's at stake.

Once, after countless hours without sleep, I managed to slip away from the steady backbeat of noise and hum of fluorescent lights into the break room to lie down for a nap. I closed my eyes and instantly felt the sweet embrace of sleep. In my dream state, I was lying on the forest floor, staring up at the mottled light, listening to the cicadas' whir, at first soft, then louder and louder, until the cicadas' whir got so loud, I awoke with a jolt. My beeper read, *Level One Trauma, Adult Male, Multiple GSW*.

Multiple gunshot wounds.

I dragged myself to my feet and shook the fatigue from my eyes. I splashed water on my face as I prepared myself for what fresh horrors awaited me in the trauma bay of the ER.

The patient was about my age—late twenties—bleeding profusely, ravaged by the profound effects that pea-sized chunks of lead moving at the speed of sound can inflict on the human body. I saw in him man's inhumanity to man and the terrible toll that drugs and gang warfare took in inner-city Baltimore. I imagined myself taking his place. In my

— 1 —

sleep-numbed state, I actually felt for a moment as if we had swapped souls. Who might I have been, and how might I have died? At the hands of others as desperate as I or by my own desperate hand?

It was a shocking revelation . . . but not entirely surprising. The strangest part was the warm familiarity of this experience. If it weren't for a few key moments and seemingly small decisions in my life, I could have been him; a select number of decisions in my life drastically changed my trajectory and outcome.

As I looked at the gunshot victim, I thought about my childhood. It was quite unlike *Leave It to Beaver* or *Father Knows Best*: no strong, wise father to talk over my problems with as he thoughtfully puffed his briar pipe; no mother's aprons to clutch onto for comfort when the world seemed too scary or painful. Neither had I come from a "broken home." My parents had stayed together throughout everything, though no one who knew anything about us would have ever called our home unbroken.

How did my parents stay together? And most importantly, why? Their relationship was wrought with upheaval, want, uncertainty, hunger, cold, and codependency. Our family's dysfunctional life was nomadic, yet anything but carefree. We moved nearly twenty times before I finished high school, nearly every move coming at the hands of landlords at the end of their patience or innkeepers raging at our door. I spent my entire senior year of high school homeless, sleeping in an old pickup truck, many nights shivering through the fierce Utah winters.

And yet here I was, prepping to save the life of a gunshot victim, privileged to be training at one of the most elite medical institutions in the country. My future shimmered with possibility.

I shook my head, trying to climb back into the moment to deal with the serious problem at hand, patching up this gunshot victim as best I could. (He would live, but his life would be forever compromised, and he would likely have scars.) I then shuffled my way to the *Christus Consolator* statue under the lobby dome at Hopkins. It was one of my favorite places in the world. That gorgeous, towering sculpture of Christ, a full-sized replica of Bertel Thorvaldsen's original, affecting with its beauty even those who do not resonate with its religious significance. The statue was a reminder of my youth, the significance of Christ to the members of my faith, and here at Hopkins, another reminder of how far He had brought me.

As I stood by the statue, I stared at the scars etched in the hands and feet of the statue. *Scars. We all have them.* When we look in the mirror, we see some of them. However, many we do not. The deep scars from the wounds that hurt the most, the wounds that fracture our souls, we hide deep in our hearts, buried, locked in a strongbox in our minds. We hope to never face them and the deep, searing pain they hold. Yet when we get the courage to open that box, face its contents, and face ourselves, we find that we can change those hidden wounds into scars. They never heal completely, but they can become strong, a significant reminder of the battles and demons that we have fought and overcome.

Then, when we can summon the strength to share these scars with others, they become even stronger and can serve as strength to lift others, to give them hope, to help them win their own victories, and earn scars for themselves in overcoming their personal battles. Scars then become badges, badges of honor that we can wear proudly, because they helped us to become stronger and molded us into who we are today.

Even to this day, when I close my eyes to rest, sometimes the nightmares from my past come in the lonely darkness, unbidden, unwelcome guests to disturb my restful sleep. But when I wake each day, the sun rises, and the nightmares fade into the shadows, scars of the past, as I embrace my pain and accept that my scars are an integral part of me.

A lasting truth is that we cannot be beaten by something we don't fear. When we are able to face the past and face our fears, not hide from those deep wounds, accept the badges of honor they have become, and accept ourselves, we can love ourselves and, in doing so, find a deepened resolve to continue to vanquish our demons and rise triumphantly at the end of the battle.

These are my scars. I share them with you so that you may use them to have hope: hope for a better life, hope for a happier life; and strength: strength to live your dreams and reach for the stars.

CHAPTER 2

Early Childhood

I was born in 1973, the sixth of what would be eleven children: eight boys, and three girls. And until I was four years old, life seemed fairly normal. Being toward the middle of the birth order was the prime place for bearing witness to the madness that was my family. I did not have my older siblings' trigger-happy tensions and conflicts with my parents, nor was I babied and coddled. It often felt that my parents made it worse for my younger siblings, trying to atone for their sins of neglect and abuse, but instead enmeshing them in cycles of dysfunction and dependency. I was happy to be in the middle, the Goldilocks position in a big family. I was happy to observe, to be left alone, and to figure things out for myself.

As with all idyllic states, it had to end. My father lost his well-paying job in the steel mill. A brilliant, quirky, unconventional man—he saw himself as a great inventor—Dad was not able to maintain a regular job, or he simply chose not to. His bosses were either idiots or thieves, taking credit for his ideas or refusing to even consider them. His coworkers were jealous and always undermining him. He never seemed to have any friends. "Great minds think alike," he told himself whenever he read of some new invention in *Popular Mechanics* or *Popular Science*, those dog-eared copies he piled up on every available surface. Then, under his breath, I'd hear him mutter the rest of the quote: "And fools seldom differ." It took me years to understand whom he was talking to.

Aside from his complaints and shortcomings, Dad was mostly level-headed. Mom on the other hand was a tinderbox. Most days she was irrational, unapproachable, and a bag of undulating emotions, like a rough sea. Her struggles—ranging from bulimia, possible bipolar disorder, anxiety, and many other clinical conditions—went undiagnosed. She was self-aggrandizing, often telling us how she was the darling of her town. Mom was a complicated woman during my childhood. I loved her with all my heart and still do, but more often than not we didn't get along and failed to see eye to eye. Her behavior strained our lives on many occasions, but I've come to accept the struggles as scars, which have molded me to become the person I am.

Perhaps not surprisingly—being from Utah—we are members of The Church of Jesus Christ of Latter-day Saints. Members of our church are often nicknamed "Mormons," yet are correctly called Latter-day Saints. Latter-day Saints are often well-known for their dietary restrictions including coffee, tea, and alcohol. Iconic missionaries of this church wear black name tags and walk in pairs through streets all over the world.

One of the church's core and unique teachings is that couples and families can live together forever in the eternities, not just 'till death do they part. This in particular had a tremendous impact on me.

BIG WHEELS

One of my first vivid memories is being four years old and in a new classroom. We were learning to jump rope. I remember the rest of the kids, their laughter sweet and genuine. Even though I was only a year younger than the others, and even though later in life I would excel in multiple sports, try as I might, I could not quite master jumping rope. I could not find the rhythm, my feet and the rope getting hopelessly tangled up, the teacher patiently untangling them for me, telling me, "That's great, Chris! You can do it!"

I felt the fear in the pit of my stomach, a sinking dread . . . fear that I would, of all things, fail kindergarten. I had learned fear from my mother and her habit of never answering the door when someone rang the bell or knocked, herding us kids into a closet, shushing us behind the couch: fear of strangers, fear of the world, fear of failure. My incompetency at jumping rope preyed upon my young mind for months until I finally learned—with relief or even more fear, depending on the day—that I had been advanced into the first grade.

I had made a friend, Aaron, a neighbor about my age, and I still had the Big Wheel that my parents (also known as Santa Claus back in those days) had given me for Christmas. Aaron also had one. These were wondrous contraptions to us at that age, vehicles that thrilled us with speed and freedom of movement for the first time in our lives. For a few months, as often as we could after the rigors of the first-grade curriculum, Aaron and I would blast about the neighborhood on our Big Wheels.

Then one afternoon, I came home from school to find a truck in our yard and strange men loading up our things (I would soon become an expert at packing things up in a hurry). My parents told me that we were moving, again, and that I'd have to say goodbye to my Big Wheel friend. I'd soon realize that true friends would be as rare as a hot meal.

We moved away in such a rush that I didn't get a chance to say goodbye to Aaron.

This scenario repeated itself many times over for most of my childhood. As a result, my brothers and I learned to play among ourselves and grew to be good friends. We started to keep more to ourselves rather than risk the pain of making friends, only to part ways soon after. Because of this, my best friends growing up were my brothers and sisters. We didn't have a lot of playthings or fancy toys, so we used our imaginations. We had a lot of fun creating and developing simple games that we would play together. We even staged our own mini-Olympics, complete with track and field events that we created. We exercised our imaginations as much as our bodies. I believe imagination is what helped us through difficulties we hated to endure but became far too accustomed to experiencing.

SKID MARKS

Being in a large family with multiple brothers and my parents not having a lot of money, we shared clothes—shirts, pants, socks, and even underwear - hand-me-downs, thrift store selections, Kmart socks by the big bundle like bales of cotton. Clothes were considered communal property, often not quite fitting right, too tight or too loose. Underwear was by *far* the least favorite part of sharing as some of them would eventually end up stained with the dreaded "skid marks." We would often end up having arguments and disagreements over who would have to wear the skid-mark-stained underwear. Tighty-whities? Rarely white—or tight, for that matter.

Typically, what would happen is that one of my younger brothers would grab the underwear first thing in the morning. And then, shortly thereafter, when one of the older siblings discovered that the only underwear remaining bore the shameful skid marks, they would use brute force to reclaim the unstained pair.

All our clothes continued to be communal property throughout most of my life growing up until I was able to purchase my own. Fortunately, despite the age differences, we were fairly close in size and just shared hand-me-downs. Usually, our shoes would be hand-me-down, Kmart closeout, or thrift store, thus not necessarily fitting properly. After all these years, my feet still bear scars and malformations from not wearing proper-fitting footgear. We made do as best we could. If we had a family crest, our motto would have been, "Make do as best you can as it could be worse." Often it did get worse before it got better.

YELLOWSTONE TRIP

When I was about six years old, my family decided to take a road trip to Yellowstone National Park. We had a brown seventies Chevy van with thick brown shag carpet and small round windows in the back. Everything went well on the trip until we started driving through the park. The rigors of the landscape in Yellowstone took its toll on the van, which started acting up and would nearly stall as it struggled up hills. It had such a difficult time that the old heap would slow to five to ten mph by the time it reached the top of a hill, and inside we feared that the engine would give out and we'd roll backward to our doom. We kids decided that when it limped slowly like that, we should all try leaning forward to build momentum to try to help the van get up the hill. So every few minutes, one of my siblings would say, "Okay, everyone lean forward!" Of course, it didn't help, but it made the time more fun.

The AC also stopped working, so it would get stiflingly hot, especially with the excess insulation of the brown shag carpet in the van. The combination of brown shag carpet and stifling heat made for a nauseating trip battling motion sickness; we held back vomit multiple times. It did make for a memorable trip, though.

THE GREEN HOUSE

A few years and several house moves later, we were living at the "Green House" in Manila, Utah—a relatively rural area in northern Utah County near Highland and Alpine—when everything changed. I was nine years old, and something happened, the type of event that defines your life as "before" and "after."

The Green House was roomy, and my parents gave me and a younger brother, Aaron, a stagecoach bed to sleep in. It had the stagecoach facade on the headboard and sides, so of course, Aaron and I played cowboys with each other for endless hours. That bed was the site of many fond memories.

Our bedroom was in the basement. One night when I went down the stairs to turn in, the entire floor was soaked, all the way into the hallway. We could not stay there without soaking ourselves and the bed. It was preposterous.

I asked Dad what was wrong, and he said, "Some plumbing issue. The drain or the septic tank is backed up." He never fixed it. I gave up sleeping down there and started sleeping on the floor in the main family room, but little did I know the flood in our basement was related to dangerous water levels outside, which caused the septic tank to overflow.

The house had a small amount of land nearby with a small hill, at the bottom of which was an irrigation ditch. The ditch was around three to four feet deep. Most of the time it was empty. During certain parts of the year, the ditch would fill with irrigation water headed for the endless orchards of cherries, peaches, and apples; the acres of beans, barley, and, my favorite, the rippling waves of wheat.

While we lived in this house, my younger brother Sammy was born. His birthday was the day after mine, eight years apart, so we had a common bond. When I was eight years old, my older brother, who was sixteen at the time, baptized me. Because I was such a thinker, I did the math, and I wanted to baptize Sammy when he turned eight and I was sixteen. We lived in this house for some time until Sammy was twenty months old, which was actually a long time for us to remain in one house.

Sammy was able to get around well. He liked to wear cowboy boots and dance to music. His favorite song was "Come On Eileen" by Dexys Midnight Runners. I loved my baby brother and loved playing with him. Some days, as older brothers do, I would tease and harass him by chasing him around the house while vacuuming. He used to love to go see the ducks in the field behind the house by the irrigation ditch. He was my little bud.

One day, my parents brought home a new game for the Atari 2600 called *Cowboy*. We sat around playing the new video game for hours, as kids are prone to do. Some of my older siblings were out of town at a three-day youth conference. While we were playing, one of us noticed that Sammy was missing. We all decided to look for him. My parents also began looking for him. I remember looking in the cupboards and cabinets, thinking he was playing hide-and-seek. At first, I was rather irritated that Sammy was hiding and wouldn't come out. We looked all over the house and still couldn't find him.

As the minutes crept by and my anxiety increased, I began saying a prayer as I walked around looking for Sammy, praying that he'd be okay, that he had ended up following a neighbor's dog or that he was hiding in a closet corner and had fallen asleep. Our parents were getting scared, which meant we kids were even more scared.

"Sammy!" I shouted.

We all shouted "Sammy!" until our voices grew hoarse.

Finally, at wit's end, my parents called the police. The officer who responded sized up the situation immediately and called for the K-9 corps. The German shepherds arrived and got straight to business. The handler held up one of Sammy's t-shirts, and off the dogs went, seasoned professionals. For a moment I felt relief; surely they would find him when we couldn't.

It was a scene seared into my brain, reappearing in nightmares for years, lasting decades. The dogs took off for the irrigation field. It was filled to capacity when I could have sworn just the day before it was dry as dust. I witnessed the commotion from the back deck, as if everything were slowed down, and the only thing that felt real was the clenching fist of dread in my stomach. The dogs scuttled back and forth on the bridge that spanned the ditch; this was where the scent faded out. The officers had a hard time inspecting under the bridge as the water was running high and muddy.

Dad couldn't stand the suspense. Without taking off his shoes or clothes, he dove under the bridge. Within seconds, he broke through the surface, clutching my baby brother's lifeless body, limp as a rag doll in his red and blue overalls, his skin pale, white as porcelain. My dad handed Sammy to the officer, holding him by one leg while the other leg and his arms hung limply. For all the world, he looked like he was deep in a dreamless sleep. It was one of those moments when I stood outside myself, looking sadly at myself standing on the porch, staring at the unfolding horror. I felt a storm of emotion coming over me like the snow clouds breaking over the Wasatch Mountains, dark and menacing, and I had no way to escape.

Not that I didn't try. I ran into the house and hid behind the couch in the tight space between the couch's arm and the wall, sobbing uncontrollably, as if a monster were trying to burst free from my stomach. It felt like hours. Then I felt a gentle hand on my shoulder, and one of the officers gave me a kind smile.

"Are you okay, son?"

He knew I wasn't.

I knew I wasn't.

"No sir, I'm sad and trying to hide."

He shook his head gently, the leather of his belt holster creaking as he reached down a hand to help me up.

"Now, son, why don't you come out here and join your brothers and sisters? You all need each other right now. You've gotta look out for each other. Your parents are at the hospital, and it might be a while before we know anything for sure."

An eternity later, the phone rang. We all looked at each other, and no one moved, until my oldest sister, Darlene, broke the suspense and snatched the phone off its cradle.

"Hello?" she said, as if she didn't know who it was.

She did. It was my parents with the news we knew was coming. The ER doctors had tried everything they could to revive Sammy, but he was too far gone. I remember little else about that day except the neighbors bringing over pans and covered dishes of casseroles and cakes, pasta, and tuna fish salad. I thought I wasn't hungry; how could I be after all that? But I was wrong. The food tasted delicious, and we all ate in silence. Words only would have sounded pitiful and wrong.

I remember people coming and going, my parents huddled up with suit-wearing strangers and suit-wearing friends from church.

A few days later, we held Sammy's funeral at the old white church in Manila. The whole town turned out. The tragedy of losing a toddler was a burden no one was expected to bear alone.

Sammy was in his casket. His curly hair was brushed neatly, and he was wearing his best white shirt and leather shoes. He looked as if he had a soft smile on his face, at peace. I suppose he was, and we were left behind to struggle on, each of us together and each of us alone.

I leaned over to kiss his forehead. The cold shock of his skin felt like marble. I had never been so close to death. Before that moment, death was an abstraction I knew people dealt with all the time, just not me. My nine-year-old self had nowhere to tuck away all those naked emotions, and I felt as if I would implode. I was strangely cold. I wanted to cry, yet there was nothing inside me but a frigid numbness.

When the funeral home director closed the casket at the end of the service, the numb feeling was replaced by a hot flush of sadness. It felt as if my hand were at my throat, choking me.

The sick sobs returned as the choir sang "Families Can Be Together Forever."

I remember thinking, *Can they? Be together? Forever?!* It sure didn't feel like it at that moment, but oh how I wanted it to be true! I cried as if my heart would burst. To this day, whenever I hear that song, the memory of that terrible day rises up like a wraith, my eyes water, and the tears fall down my cheek.

During the ride to the cemetery, I tried desperately to distract myself, counting telephone poles, noticing the wind rippling through the wheat field, feeling the soft leather of the seats of the hearse with its polished walnut trim. It was the nicest car I'd ever ridden in. But no matter how hard I tried to stay in the moment, I felt the terrible certainty that Sammy's death had been my fault.

I stared at his little coffin sitting behind me in the car, and as tears swelled my eyes, I whispered, "I'm sorry, little brother. I should be in that box instead of you. I will miss you." I told myself that it was my fault. *My fault!* I screamed in my mind. He was my little bud, and I should have protected him from all harm.

I had failed.

I had failed, and because of my failure, Sammy was gone—cold, buried in the harsh, unforgiving ground. I was never to see him grow up, never to share adventures with him. I felt as cold inside as his skin had felt to me, lost, lonely, and broken; a barren wasteland, devoid of light and joy, full of sadness and darkness.

I desperately wanted to swap places with my little brother, be in the cold box, and exchange my life for his so I could hear his laughter, see his bright smile and twinkling eyes again.

After the funeral, my mother, her beautiful curly blond hair matted and streaked with sweat, shouted at us, "You should have watched him! You shouldn't have been playing video games!"

She knew as soon as those hard words fell from her lips that she would never be able to take them back. But she tried.

"I'm sorry, sorry. It's not your fault! It was a terrible accident. Please don't think it was your fault."

My brothers and sisters looked at each other with fear in our eyes. We felt the truth of what she had said, each of us alone and each of us together.

I blamed myself for Sammy's death for many years. As I have gotten older, I realize that no one is to blame, and sometimes terrible things happen for which we don't know the reason. We are left only to learn to live with a hole in our hearts, filled with a deep, deep scar. As Hemingway wrote, "The world breaks everyone and afterward many are strong in the broken places."

My grieving parents, already struggling with a complicated world, looked haggard and defeated after Sammy's death. Dad lost another job. Mom would go days sometimes without getting out of bed. Following the loss, our already tenuous hold on financial stability slipped. Just to keep ourselves fed, my siblings and I found jobs: babysitting, mowing lawns, collecting cans, whatever we could do to earn a nickel. At the ripe old age of nine, I entered the workforce, picking cherries, peaches, apples, and other fruit at our neighbor's orchard. I pondered many times on the terrible paradox that the same canal that had taken away my brother's life gave life to the fruitful trees I tended.

I don't remember how much I got paid, but it seemed a princely sum at the time. I took some of the money I earned and bought GI Joe action figures and a GI Joe jeep. I couldn't think of anything that seemed a wiser purchase. It gave me something to do besides obsess over Sammy's death and what I felt was my part in it.

DARLENE, THE LIBRARY, AND MUSIC

After Sammy died, Mom, never the highest functioning person around, shut down completely. In her grief, she couldn't rouse the energy to get out of bed for days at a time, surrounding herself with mounds of crumpled Kleenex, racked with sobs at all hours. That was when my sister Darlene stepped in as a surrogate mother for me and the younger siblings. Darlene is petite, barely five feet tall, but she was a giant to us in her caring and compassion.

Darlene was my older sister, the nurturing mother figure of the family, oldest of all of the children, kind and compassionate. She had been forced to become responsible well beyond her years, taking it upon herself to be our little mother. She was eighteen and would drive us to various locations: school, sports, library, and other events. She would dutifully take us to the small old stone library in Pleasant Grove.

The library was in an old historic stone building, maybe twenty by thirty feet, and had a slightly musty smell. This was one of my favorite places to visit. As soon as I entered its cool darkness, the bleached, bright outside world fell into a hush in the hallowed space. I could feel my growing excitement as I scanned the rows of shelves, each containing worlds for me to discover, to explore, to shed the constant dread of not knowing when and where we would be next, where I would be uprooted to. This vault of limitless knowledge and imagination became my safe space, my home, a stable place where I imagined and learned of a world with unlimited potential for freedom and hope.

As I grew up in elementary school and throughout my later years, libraries continued to be my safe space. Books and reading were my escape.

Each week in school when we had library time, I felt as if I were exploring new worlds. When I read classic works such as C. S. Lewis's *Chronicles of Narnia* or Jules Verne or Tolkien, I was transported to new realities where there was hope, romance, and glory. When I read, I imagined a world of magnificent potential, where magical places and people existed; lands where fairies and dragons roamed, untamed, free to be themselves, to live, and to dream. I also read biographies of historical figures who overcame adversity such as Helen Keller's challenge of being blind and deaf. I read of Julius Caesar and how he turned his epilepsy into a powerful tool, as if the gods themselves had chosen him as their special messenger.

One of my favorites was Aesop's fables. I relished the wisdom imparted by the simple parables. I also liked to envision myself in the books I read, fighting alongside Aragorn against Sauron, or standing with Aslan against evil, doing what was right despite overwhelming opposition.

Reading opened my eyes and showed me the potential of people. It gave me a wider view of the world than I knew. I also learned the stories of people fighting against adversity and overwhelming odds, and learning that even though life may seem bleak, there is always hope for a better world.

I was a voracious reader. I read at least one or two books a week when I was in elementary and junior high school. The librarians all knew me by name and greeted me brightly every time I came in to exchange one stack of books for another.

Music was also my escape. Listening to music with my Sony Walkman, which I purchased from a kind lady at her garage sale, provided me a way to express those difficult feelings and emotions that I struggled to identify and understand. I would listen to everything from Metallica to the Mormon Tabernacle Choir, even enjoying Broadway musicals. It all seemed to bypass my anxious, depressed mind and go straight into the emotional centers of my brain, where it helped me deal with the maelstrom of emotions that filled me.

The complex emotions that arose with the uncertainty and stress of my life and the emotional baggage it created were difficult to understand and face for a boy of my age. Rather than work through them, I learned to hide them from myself and the world, burying them deep in a locked box in my mind.

CHAPTER 3

Later Childhood

THE BROKEN-DOWN CAR

When I was around ten years old, my parents announced one day that we were going to go to Disneyland. That was a big day, and we danced around in a circle.

"We're going to Disneyland! We're going to Disneyland!" I could not wait to ride Pirates of the Caribbean and Space Mountain. My sisters wanted to get pictures taken with all the Disney characters—Mickey and Minnie, Pluto, and Goofy—while we all wanted to ride the Monorail.

We could hardly believe our luck as Disneyland might as well have been on the other side of the moon. Aside from the occasional road trip such as to Yellowstone, our parents never took our huge brood anywhere. Too expensive, too much work.

Mom was just as excited as we were. It felt like—finally—the veil of sadness was lifting from her after Sammy's death. Dad said it would take two days of driving; then we would stay several days before returning home. It was far and away the biggest trip we'd ever taken.

The night before we left, I could hardly sleep, imagining all the rides and attractions, from the Main Street Electrical Parade to the costumes, food, and fun.

We started heading south along Interstate 15, and the first few hours were pretty uneventful—just farms and high desert rolling by on the northern Utah plateau. We were about three hours south of Provo in a town called Beaver when the engine started making a high whirring noise, which got louder and louder. I somehow hoped that Dad would be able to fix it himself, but the smoke and steam curling out from underneath the hood left us with little hope.

We found an auto shop, and the mechanic, wiping the sweat from his forehead with a greasy towel, gave Dad the bad news. "I can fix it, but it'll take three to four days to get the parts in. And another day to fix it. You got anywhere to stay?"

"No," my father said. The discouraging tone in his voice made all our shoulders slump.

The mechanic suggested an inexpensive hotel in Beaver. At least it had a pool. That was where we spent most every waking hour. We made the most of it. The rest of the guests might have found the boisterous crew a little too noisy for their tastes, but everyone had the kindness to keep that to themselves. My back got so sunburned it blistered. I can still feel the cool sting of Mom applying aloe vera to the peeling patches, feeling as close to her as I had since the tragedy. But Beaver, Utah was 486 miles from Disneyland and felt much farther.

Our car was fixed and we proceeded on, but our troubles weren't over. We got pulled over by a highway patrolman an hour out of Beaver, who told us that Dad's inspection and registration had expired. Dad got an expensive ticket, which on top of the expensive repairs meant we had officially burned through the rest of our money. We returned home, never reaching the Magic Kingdom, disappointed but glad at least to have made it back home intact rather than getting stuck in Beaver, Utah permanently.

BRANDON'S BIRTHDAY

It was hard to make friends when we moved around so much, but not impossible. I learned early on that some people are just nicer than others. Maybe some kids are shy; maybe they don't like newcomers interfering with the tight circles of friends they've had all their lives; maybe they're afraid their friends would like us more. But some kids welcomed us warmly, hospitably, and with open hearts.

Brandon Fugal was one such kid. I could tell where he had learned to be so nice as soon as I met his family: the way his father asked me if I needed anything, the way his mother treated me like an honored guest. Brandon and I met in fifth grade and would occasionally play Dungeons & Dragons at recess, at least until our school banned it in the 1980s.

Later in the school year, Brandon invited me to his birthday party, along with about twenty other kids. It was very exciting for me, a rare treat, and I brought him a GI Joe action figure as a gift, still in the box, one I had purchased with my own cherry-picking money. When I arrived, the guests were all running around the backyard, noisy and merry, and it felt good to be with other kids and to feel accepted and welcome. A table was adorned with birthday decorations. My GI Joe didn't look at all out of place. It was a beautiful sunny day.

We decided to break into teams and play at being ninjas. Brandon had a collection of Chinese throwing stars, and we threw them against the wooden backyard fence, trying to get them to *thunk* into the wood with enough force to stick. Every so often they would. We would also clamber over objects like the teeter-totter and his father's sawhorses like proper ninjas. Just as we were running out of energy from all the high-spirited play, Brandon's mother brought out a beautifully decorated birthday cake. We sang "Happy Birthday" with tuneless enthusiasm as Brandon blew out the candles.

At that moment, I felt as happy as I could ever imagine—to be surrounded by friends, to witness a loving, stable, dare I say *normal* family in action. That moment was like a snapshot I carried around in my memory—a perfect ideal of what I wanted for my life for my children when I was older and what I wanted to provide for them.

TWELFTH BIRTHDAY

A few years and several different houses passed by, the usual moves every few months after being evicted or asked to move. Shortly after my twelfth birthday, we moved into what we called "the Pink House," although Mom often referred to it as "the Joker House," which was a pejorative reference to the landlord, whom she felt looked like the Joker from *Batman*. She also used the slanderous term to justify her outrage when the landlord came seeking the rent owed to him.

The house wasn't nearly large enough for our whole brood, so Dad marched my brother, Johnny, and me outside to an unfinished carport. He raised his palm to it, displaying the sad outbuilding as a model might proudly show off an exotic car.

"This is where you and your brother will sleep," he announced.

Johnny and I stared at the carport for a moment, at the bare two-by-fours, only occasionally concealed by jagged chunks of drywall, at the bare concrete floor, the tangles of spiderwebs. Then we turned to each other, mouths agape. It wasn't as though we had become accustomed to living in luxury, but even for us, this seemed a space not quite fit for human habitation.

I asked, "Is there any heat?"

Dad scratched his head as though he had never thought of that before. "I guess not." Then he shrugged, like *No big deal.* "We'll get you a space heater of some kind. You're boys. You'll be fine."

With that, he turned on a heel and headed back for the house. We took his word for it. After all, winter was a month or so away yet, and what choice did we have?

I attempted to exude optimism. "At least we can fit the bed in here!"

"And my fish tank," Johnny said.

"And we'll finally get some peace and quiet."

Considering that there were nearly a dozen of us, peace and quiet was no small consideration. Had the place been truly habitable, it would have been a great little home away from home for Johnny and me.

But it was not habitable, and winter soon blew in with galoshes on.

Being awakened by the cold in the early morning can be harsh. I realized that I was shivering. My face was icy, and fog billowed from my mouth.

"Johnny?" I called out. "It's freezing in here!"

He stirred, then groaned, then sat bolt upright. "My fish!"

He jumped from the bed and darted to the tank. "It's frozen! It's frozen!"

"Like, solid?"

He sniffled, the tears coming. "They're dead!"

I hopped up. "Are you sure? Hard to tell with fish. Sometimes when it gets cold, they just stop moving . . . to preserve their energy, I guess."

But there was no question that at least some of his guppies, floating belly up under the sheet of ice that covered the surface of the tank, were dead. Johnny hung his head. My heart hurt for him, but there was little I could do to console him.

After that incident, Dad managed to scrounge up a kerosene space heater, and life inside the carport improved . . . a bit. We *were* boys, after all, kids, and we found our toughness and resiliency whenever and wherever we could. We found it because we had no other choice. Many evenings, we got into animated discussions that lasted long into the night, some of it nonsense, some of it juvenile existentialism, but all of it huddled within an arm's length of that heater.

DIGGING UP PHONE LINES

One day after school, I headed into the Pink House and grabbed our phone so I could call my buddy, Jim Clark. The phone line was dead. I heard Mom banging around in the kitchen, so I called out, "Mom! The phone isn't working!"

"Yeah? I guess the phone company guys were digging around and cut the lines. Hopefully, it'll be working again in a few days."

With our already checkered history of moving from place to place, outrunning landlords, and attempting to outmaneuver utility companies, I thought that seemed a reasonable explanation. I was still willing to give my parents the benefit of the doubt.

But a few days later, I came home from school to find the house unusually dark inside, and within a few moments, my siblings and I realized that there was no power. The explanation from my mother: "Oh! I think the phone company was digging around and cut some cables or wires or something like that. It'll probably work again soon. We can have a cold dinner tonight."

Even before moving into the Pink House, we'd had many cold dinners—if there was one that in any way aligned with the definition of *dinner*. So that was nothing unusual. But upon hearing the same explanation about utilities from my mother the second time, we knew that something was amiss, not with trench-digging contractors but with our family's meager

CHRISTOPHER L. SMITH, M.D.

finances. Despite the repetition of that story about the phone company for both the telephone and the power outage, we could find no holes or trenches anywhere in the neighborhood that would explain what had happened.

Of course, we kids had no choice but to carry on. School was our distraction, our haven, and there was homework to be done. So we got a fire going in the fireplace and huddled as close as we possibly could and dared to, and we used flickering, feeble light to complete our studies before bedtime, which would be even colder than usual without heat of any kind.

Aaron, ever the optimist, having learned in school how when our six-teenth president was a boy, he'd scratch out his sums with a chunk of char-coal on a shovel blade, said, "If Abraham Lincoln could do it, so can we!"

As it turned out, we would be without utilities not for days but months.

Nevertheless, we had to bathe occasionally lest we appear to the world the filthy ragamuffins that we actually were. At least the water still worked.

My siblings and I concocted a process for heating water over the fire-place in pots and pans, then trudging it over to the bathtub. It was serious work and took quite a bit of time, and soon we realized that we needed to reuse the same bathwater during bath time. Naturally, the water grew dingier and cooler with each child. All of us would shout "Dibs!" but con-siderable differences of opinion about who had shouted dibs first led to near brawls. And those of us who found ourselves the last to bathe took to griping about it with great enthusiasm.

One evening, I hustled into the bathroom just as my brother Tom was climbing out of the tub. The water was so dingy and oil-slicked that it had lost most of its resemblance to water at all.

"What were you doing before you got in the tub?" I shouted. "Rolling in pig slop?"

"It wasn't me! It was already disgusting when I got into it!"

"I'll just get dirtier if I get in there."

"Well, don't get in there!"

When Tom marched out of the bathroom, I folded my arms, staring at the mud puddle that was to be my bath, determined to take a stand and not bathe at all. But I knew that fetid tub would be better than no bath at all. Goodness knows how long before I could get a proper bath. I got out of my clothes and cringed as I put one foot in that cold cesspool, then the other. I finally managed to work up enough nerve to sit down in it and grab what was left of the soap and attempt to clean myself up.

These rituals would be repeated week after week, with no relief in sight.

Then it was time for dinner. Not cold tonight. Cooked, so to speak, by Mom over the fireplace. As she handed the plates around, we all held them close, squinting, attempting to figure out what was under the pool of gravy.

I decided to ask.

Mom said, "Tuna fish gravy over tater tots."

All of us, me included, were fine with tuna, or tater tots, or even gravy. But all at once? I suppose it could be described as an "interesting" combination of flavors in a bland yet clashing way. The smell tended to induce a bit of nausea, but what else could you do except eat it? As anyone who's had to eat whatever is available to survive would attest, it was better than nothing . . . which I can say with authority because that was exactly what we would have the next night: nothing.

While eating unusual food combinations such as tuna fish gravy over tater tots, I discovered one of the secrets of the universe, that ketchup can make almost anything taste better, even tuna fish gravy. I started experimenting with different foods in combination with ketchup. Potato chip sandwiches with ketchup, I told myself, were "not too bad!" Add a few pickles and grated parmesan cheese and it became a "balanced meal" with "vegetables and dairy"! (At least that is what my young mind told myself.) Ketchup became my go-to necessary condiment; I started putting it on everything to make food palatable.

While money was always scarce, Mom's mental condition—whether best diagnosed as bipolar disorder, obsessive-compulsive disorder, or borderline personality disorder—was all over the map when it came to managing what little cash we had. At times she seemed hesitant to spend a penny, even when we had no food and heat. Other times she would rush off and, in an extravagant way, blow it all on clothing for herself. Her bulimia gave her a characteristically split personality towards food. Often, she wouldn't eat even when we had food. Other times she would stuff herself with all the food available in the household, leaving her children without a crumb, and then rush to the bathroom and vomit it all up. I did love my mother; I just didn't understand her and her condition.

Many years later as I went through medical school, I learned that treatment might have helped Mom live a better life, and I wish she would have sought help for her condition, for her and for us, her children. I deeply wished I could have helped her seek treatment, but as a child, I did not know what to do to help her. If anyone who reads this has similar problems, I urge you to seek treatment.

SPORTS

I played basketball when I was younger. I loved the game, the rhythm and the fast pace of it, but most of all the thrilling sound when the ball swished through the net. One scene in particular sticks out in my mind. When we were living in the Pink House (the Joker House), my parents dropped me off at the gym for practice. As I walked in, I saw my team lined up neatly in our green Junior Jazz jerseys. I had some solid friends on the team (Chris Lee and Derek Robinson especially) and waved at them. They waved back. It felt good to be part of a team, to know these people were on your side.

We weren't the best team, though. In fact, we were often comically bad. But our lack of skill didn't stop us from enjoying ourselves. We had plenty of fun. More importantly, I had friends who accepted me for who I was without any pretense.

As we went through our drills, we practiced dribbling; making sharp, clean passes; free throws; and working on good form for our jump shots. I liked playing forward or center, to post up under the basket to go after rebounds. I thought if I worked on boxing out my opponents underneath the basket, I could get rebounds through hard work and discipline. It didn't matter if the other guy was taller or more athletic. If I did my job, he couldn't do his. I felt I would then be an important asset to the team, contributing to whatever success we achieved.

After drills, we broke into different teams for a scrimmage. It was intense and we were running up and down the court, sweating and going all out as if it were the championship. My friend Kary Johansson went up for a shot, and I jumped to try to block it. He came forward into me with the momentum of his shot, and his head struck me underneath my chin. I remember a burst of light and then . . . nothing. I came to, lying on the court with my worried teammates circling me. As the daze faded and my blurry vision sharpened, I saw that the top of Kary's head was bleeding, and I realized my tooth was chipped. Apparently, I had been knocked out cold for several minutes. Kary got multiple stitches in his scalp, and I was diagnosed by the school nurse with a mild concussion.

After practice concluded so dramatically and we prepared to leave, my parents were not there waiting for me with the other parents. Several of my friends asked if I needed a ride home. My pride made me decline.

"No thanks. I'm sure my parents got tied up somewhere. They'll be here soon," I said with little confidence.

My coach waited with me until he had to leave and turned out the lights in the gym. I had to wait outside. I waited for an hour by myself, bouncing the basketball off the school's wall.

Eventually, I decided my parents weren't coming to get me, and I walked home. It was two miles. The sun was setting, and darkness was settling in rapidly. The road was a two-lane highway without many stoplights but with, fortunately, a sidewalk for most of the way. I made the most of the journey, practicing my dribbling. When I finally arrived home, I saw the car in the driveway and wondered, *Why didn't they come to get me?*

I walked in, and my parents greeted me as if nothing out of the ordinary had happened.

I told them, "Practice was great. We've got a big game coming up Friday, and we might have a chance to win."

It slowly dawned on Dad that he had forgotten to pick me up.

He looked away from the television set and rubbed his brow with his hand as he sighed. "I'm sorry, son. I had to pick up your sister at dance practice and just forgot."

That wasn't the first time. It wouldn't be the last. In his defense, there were a lot of us kids, and he wasn't the most detail-oriented guy.

At least Dad encouraged me to play sports. It was my saving grace. When I was twelve, Dad decided I should start playing baseball. I was upset because I was introverted, and the idea of joining a bunch of strangers to play a sport I knew little about was terrifying. When we arrived at the park, I ran and hid behind the batting cage to avoid practice. It was not my proudest moment. Soon, though, I realized I had a natural ability for the sport and ended up loving it. That first year I ended up leading the league in home runs. The team bonded, and I felt that I had a new family on the baseball diamond.

Near the end of the season, we had an important game coming up against one of the league's top teams. I went with my older brother Darwin to pick up my friend Jim Clark to bring him to my house before the game. It was a nice sunny Saturday. I was in the back seat of the car, a small red, two-door Ford Escort. Jim was in the front. When we arrived back at my house, he let the seat down so I could get out. I reached up to grab the door edge for leverage. At that moment, not knowing I was still climbing out, Jim shut the door. Unfortunately, my third finger on my right hand was still on the doorjamb, but he used such force that the door completely shut despite my finger being in the way. I remember a few seconds when I didn't feel anything . . . except dread, knowing that the pain would soon come. And so it did, in big throbs that left me dizzy and afraid I would pass out. My finger was still stuck in the shut door. Darwin, usually quite calm, freaked out and yanked the door open with great force. When he did, it ripped the nail completely off my finger, leaving a bloody pulp.

The funny thing is that I didn't cry, even through the blinding pain. I put on a brave face.

I think my stoic attitude really began with Sammy's death. Life is hard, and complaining about it doesn't make it easier. Terrible things happen, and all you can control is the way you react to circumstance. There's no point in showing emotion and weakness; people will just use them against you. Put on a mask and soldier through it.

While this defense mechanism did protect me against pain, it also shut out other people and never allowed them to get to know my authentic self: my vulnerabilities, my tender side. I also never worked through the pain to turn the wound into a scar. The pain was there, and I felt it deeply; otherwise, I wouldn't go to such great effort to hide it. But my parents taught me that people were always out to get us and that we couldn't trust anyone. So I learned to not trust anyone, including myself, and hid some of the best parts of me.

Anyway, after my finger was smashed in the door, my parents took me to the emergency room, and I got an X-ray. Miraculously, nothing was broken. I got stitches in my nail bed and a large bandage over my finger. I still have the scar.

We still had a game that day.

Dad said, "Son, you can't play in your condition. If you like, you can sit on the bench to cheer on your team. Maybe the coach's wife can teach you how to keep score."

"No, Dad," I said with determination through the throbs of pain, "I'm going to play. This is the biggest game of the season so far, and *no way* am I going to miss it!"

He shrugged. "Okay, it's your call. But no one is going to think less of you if you sit this one out."

The rest of the team gasped as they saw me waving my bandage around like a foam finger. Go team!

Jim told me in front of everyone, "It was my fault. But look at Chris; he's fierce! Didn't slow him down for a minute. If he's so sure he can play, then what's our excuse? We'd better play the best we've played all season!"

His little pep talk worked. We played as good a game as we'd played all season. I could still hold the ball and throw pretty well even with the bandage on. The coach switched me from center field to second base, though; he was afraid if I had to make a long throw from the outfield, the bandage would fly off.

It was hard to grip the bat but not impossible. My first at-bat, I hit a weak fly to right field. But the second at-bat, I figured out that if I twisted the bat around to protect my bandaged finger, I could compensate with a sturdier grip with my left hand. The pitcher threw hard, with surprising velocity for someone so young, but I was ready. The pitch was low and away, hard to hit for most anyone else. But that was my sweet spot. I turned on the pitch, and as soon as the bat connected with the ball, it made that satisfying *pock* sound, which meant a clean, hard-hit ball. It lofted over the left field fence so far, the fielder didn't even bother running after it. I circled the bases, holding up my bandaged finger in celebration.

Go team indeed!

PANCAKES AND ICE CREAM

Jim Clark was one of the best friends I've ever had. His father, Bill Clark, was our baseball coach. We bonded over baseball, and Jim used to invite me to his house all the time. He seemed to understand without saying anything that I was in no situation to reciprocate with my messy, uncertain circumstances at home. His parents were wonderful. His mother's sweet smile made me feel instantly at home, such a contrast to my mother's fickle moods and often dour demeanor.

One night I slept over, and we had the kind of fun only rambunctious eleven- and twelve-year-old boys can, playing video games, playing Dungeons & Dragons, playing catch in the backyard, and watching the movie *Goonies* on TV. After talking all night about our hopes and dreams, we fell asleep midsentence, exhausted by the glorious day behind us.

In the morning, we woke up and shuffled into the kitchen. Jim's parents had made these beautiful, thin, crêpe-like pancakes. They also had a carton of ice cream sitting on the table. For all the weird combinations of slop my mother would feed us, this was new to me.

Mr. Clark said, "Chris, this is one of our family traditions. We put ice cream on our pancakes for special occasions, and it's special to have you as our guest."

Mr. Clark knew exactly what to say to make me feel like an honored guest. I distinctly recall thinking, *One day I'm going to have my own family traditions. Maybe it will be pancakes with ice cream, maybe something else, but this right here? This is how you build a family culture.*

WALKING ALONE ALONG THE CANAL

Living in the Pink House and rooming with my brother Johnny in the freezing carport, I easily felt depressed. If you didn't, there'd have to have been something wrong with you, you know? I thought of happy times with little brother Sammy, his infectious laugh, and his joyful dancing to "Come On Eileen."

I was only eleven when these dark moods would overtake me, so I'd go walking alone along the dirt road that ran alongside the Murdock irrigation canal by the house, looking far out over the smooth surface of the dark water, watching it flow from the mountains to the fields of wheat and barley, the cherry and apple orchards down below. Sometimes I'd be gone for several hours, seeking some consolation for my sadness. Walking along the canal road was the closest to any kind of therapy I'd received: the sun, the fresh air, just being away from the madness of our life. It would usually make me feel better. I would have these incessant dialogues with myself, fantasizing about how I was going to escape these crazy circumstances, to become something true and good in the world. I imagined myself being like my hero, Aragorn, overcoming insurmountable odds to achieve the impossible.

At these times, I would also converse with God, asking Him for help, and it felt as if I received it. *Be brave; carry on; you can do it. Anything is possible with my love*, God would say to me. I felt close to Him and His creation. The ugliness of my surroundings would suddenly become beautiful—a sunset, a reminder of the beauty in the world, as though the light broke through my dark moods—and I would return home ready to face anything.

Looking Back

Looking back, I find it odd that my parents never worried about me no matter how long I was gone, sometimes for many hours. I'd return, and it would be as if I had never left. Mom would be scrounging up pennies from her pocketbook, muttering angrily to herself, while Dad would look over his newspaper at me, unaware I had even left. This went on for a few years at the Pink House in Manila, Utah.

When I was twelve, the miserable weight of my existence felt unbearable. I searched for ways to escape. I thought about how if I could just summon up the courage to commit suicide, I could finally be free. What shocked me most was the startling clarity of these thoughts, as if the usual going-through-the-motions of home, school, sports, and church were some kind of illusion, a cruel delusion that I produced myself.

For my twelfth birthday, I was given a 20-gauge shotgun, an old single-shot for hunting birds, mostly pheasants. Dad and I would stalk through the foothills, waiting for the noisy rush as the ring-necked birds would erupt from the brushy cover. I'd patiently swing the gun barrel just ahead of the bird, just as Dad had taught me, and pull the trigger steadily so that it often came as a surprise when the cartridge would blast out the #5 or #6 birdshot pellets. I was a decent shot, and if I missed, my father would be right behind me, his barrel trained just ahead of the bird, ready to knock it out of the sky. Those pheasants stood little chance.

It felt great to bag a bird or sometimes two, to provide a delicious dinner for our hungry family. My dad and I would pluck the feathers and clean the birds, saving the gizzards for the stockpot. Dad would parboil off the pinfeathers, rub the bird with salt and pepper and other spices, then roast it until the delicious smell would fill the house. It was about as happy as I'd see my dad, in his power as a father teaching his son how to hunt.

DEEPENING SCARS

We'd moved at least a half-dozen times in six years, and I was sick of it: the shame, the uncertainty, the cold and hunger. I'd lost so many friends over the years that I began to fear I'd never make another, that I'd forever be an outcast, the weird kid with the weird family with the thrift store, hand-me-down, ill-fitting clothes.

On my darkest days, I began to lose my faith in God, that maybe He'd made some kind of mistake, that maybe He'd sent me to this place by some accident. Maybe I'd been born into the wrong family and that there was a kid living with a normal family that had been meant for me. I'd imagine this impostor's life down to the last detail: the birthday parties; the laughter of his friends; his latest new clothes and bicycle, even a motorbike; his cheerful mom and steady, reliable father. Did that kid ever wonder if he was living someone else's life? I doubted it.

This self-talk always led me down a dark path. I wondered if anyone would ever notice if I was gone. It was a terrible, sad thought, but I wondered if my parents even really missed Sammy, his dancing, his joyful energy. It shocked me how quickly everyone had gotten back to our strange normal patterns. Mom was never the same, true, but it wasn't as if she had been a model of perfection to begin with. I would often lie on my bed, staring up at the old shotgun, its weathered stock and pitted barrel, thinking about how quickly everything could be over. If only I had the courage to just do it and stop thinking about it. Stop thinking about everything. To escape to oblivion.

I grabbed the gun off the wall. The barrel felt much colder than I expected. Hard, unforgiving. Like my life. It felt real, so much more real than this nightmare I was living. I held it for long minutes, contemplating my death. How simple would it be? One pull of the trigger and it would be over.

After a while, I began to notice the shadows creeping up the wall as the sun was setting. I rose from the bed and opened the drawer where I kept the shotgun shells. I cracked open the shotgun and fed a cartridge into the chamber.

Again, I contemplated the dark void of my life. *C'mon, you chicken! It'll be easy*, I told myself. *Just do it and get it over with!*

I turned the gun around and put it in my mouth. It was an awkward reach, but I could do it. The metallic taste wasn't as bad as I'd expected, about like sucking on a penny, cold as ice. I slowly and deliberately leaned back against the wall while sitting on the bed. Just as I mustered up the resolve to pull the trigger, that incessant dark voice in my head went still . . . deathly still.

But then I had a thought. *You are a child of God. You are important to this world. There's a lot you have left to do. There is no easy way out. There is only through. And through* God's love, *everything, anything, is possible.*

Tears started running down my cheeks—hot tears. I sobbed until I fell asleep. Sometime later, in the dark of night, I awoke and placed the shotgun carefully back on the rack, and went into the house to rustle up some food.

I have never told anyone about this event until now. I lived with it quietly, another scar etched deep in my soul. I share this scar with you so that anyone reading this story who may find themselves in a similar dark space can know that you are not alone. Others have felt this way, and if you are in this dark place, please reach out to someone for help. Life will not always be this way; there is hope.

CHAPTER 4

Middle School and High School

MY FATHER

D ad had many faults—too many to list here. But one positive trait that countered many negative ones was that he kept us involved in sports: coaching, cheering for us, helping us master difficult skills such as throwing a tight spiral, or teaching us the proper grip for a curveball. When I was little, he coached me in soccer, then baseball, then, when I reached middle school, football.

My older brother, Darwin, also coached, along with friends of his. All were recent high school graduates. Our team was called the Steelers. I was on the kickoff team, sprinting down the field as fast as I could to tackle the returner before he could even get started upfield. We were a solid team, in no small part because of Darwin's coaching, drilling us on the fundamentals of the game (blocking and tackling especially; he believed it didn't matter how sophisticated your plays were if you couldn't execute the basics). In fact, we went undefeated two years in a row.

In one game against our main rivals, we kicked off, and the returner broke two of our tackles and was breaking away in an open field for a touchdown. I was lying back in the coverage for just such a situation. I sprinted across the field at a perfect angle and came in low, just as Darwin had coached us, and hit the runner so hard that we both ended up doing a 360-degree flip and went rolling on the field, a ball of blurry jerseys and cleats. The fans cheered, Dad louder than anyone. I had never felt faster, and now I could see that I had made Dad proud as he beamed with excitement, loudly cheering from the sidelines.

In eighth grade, we fought hard every game until we had only one game left, and that was the league championship. It's hard to put into words what it means to be on a team, even a team that loses. The bonds between your teammates are deep and true, and you'd do anything for these guys. They've got your back, and you've got theirs . . . even the ones who are annoying.

We decided, with much enthusiasm, that for the big game, we were going to make a statement of solidarity and all get flattop haircuts with our jersey numbers shaved into the sides of our heads like our hero Brian Bosworth, the All-American linebacker with the Oklahoma Sooners. So a handful of us shaved our numbers in our hair and then painted them with black eye paint prior to the big game. My number was 65, which I chose because that was Darwin's number during his stellar high school career. I was an end on defense, and on the other side of the ball, I was one of the horses up front on the offensive line. We ended up winning that championship, but whether our haircuts had anything to do with it, we'll never know. I like to think they did. That's my story and I'm sticking to it, just as our teammates stuck with one another all throughout that glorious season.

ACADEMIC AWARDS

School wasn't just sports all the time, though. I also enjoyed school classes. It was an orderly world with instructions, blackboards, and chalk. Things were either correct or not. School was a place where I could make sense of the chaos of my world. It was stable, never changing, and with clear expectations. The school didn't move unexpectedly. It was one of my safe places. I truly felt happy in school, one of the few places where I did. I loved to learn. Often, rather than watch TV or movies, I would read the encyclopedia for fun. Excelling academically was one area of my life I could control. If I put the work in, I could do well. In my young brain, effort equaled results: predictable, manageable, simple. People were happy to see me, and my teachers believed in me. They saw my potential and helped me to believe in myself. It was a world away from the chaos of my home life, where I always felt that one wrong move was going to end in failure, either with Mom screaming and cursing or Dad complaining how the world was against us.

After ninth grade, the school held an academic awards ceremony. They kept calling out my name for one award or recognition after another until it was too much for a socially awkward teen. I cringed knowing that Bryce, Mark, and my other friends were snickering as I passed by on the aisle. "Smarty-pants," "teacher's pet," I heard them whisper, loud enough for everyone in the vicinity to hear.

I believe school is easier for kids who like to socialize, not for boys who come from dysfunctional families and who try to avoid the limelight—kids like me who would rather curl up with Tolkien than watch TV, kids like me whose best friends and heroes were characters such as Gandalf and Yoda. Don't get me started. Some kids loved the social flow of school life, but not me. I tried to downplay my academic abilities and innate love of learning to avoid being harassed by my peers for standing out, for excelling. My goal was to fade into the woodwork and not be noticed, to be the nice quiet kid from the odd family.

Part of it was the way school was taught, not rewarding kids' natural curiosity but instead teaching us to fit in and get along.

At the ceremony, my history teacher got up to announce an award. He said, "This is a very special award. In fact, I've been teaching for more than twenty-five years, and I have never given any student this award. No one student has ever earned a perfect score in my class . . . until this year."

I looked around. It had to be Katie Householder, the teacher's pet: always sitting up front so she could jump up to help Mr. Farnsworth clear the blackboard, happily clapping the erasers together to knock off the old chalk. So annoying. Or it had to be Mike—so quiet, so intense you could almost feel the heat rising off him as he furiously filled in the circles on the tests, always the first to turn it in as if it were a race.

Don't get me wrong; I loved history: the ancient Greeks fighting off a Persian army five times their size at the Battle of Marathon, or how Napoleon conquered all of Europe, though I particularly loved reading about how he had been inspired by George Washington's ability to move an army with great speed, or the westward expansion, how America became the greatest nation on Earth because of that pioneer spirit, always wanting to see what's around the next bend of the river or beyond the next mountain. These historical figures were my mentors and my friends. I wanted to be like them. I believe we as a society can't know where we're going if we don't know where we've been.

In any event, I knew I had done well in the class, but I almost fell out of my chair when my name was announced. I walked down the aisle. There was no snickering by either Bryce or Mark this time. I rarely felt more awkward as my fellow students clapped. You could tell they were sincere in their enthusiasm . . . at least some of them. All the time through school, though, I still felt that I was going to fail every grade, be held back, and that I was hanging my head in shame. Inside I silently told myself, *I'm never going to be good enough; I'll always need to be better.* It was years before I heard of "impostor syndrome." But when I did, I instantly recognized the diagnosis.

In my college psychology class, the professor asked, "You know who doesn't have impostor syndrome? Impostors." That made me feel a little more secure later in my life.

AP HISTORY REBELLION

A few years after the big surprise of the award, the school placed me in as many Advanced Placement courses as were available. These were college-level courses given to the best and brightest high school students (at least so they said) in order to keep them challenged and engaged.

In eleventh grade, the goal of AP History was to take the national test. If you passed it, you got college credit. I was running the table, earning an A on every assignment. But my mother was relentless in her criticism.

"What? How'd you get three wrong on that test?" she'd practically shriek at me. "My goodness, are you on drugs? Is that why you're doing so poorly?" She would become accusatory, having just read in one of her magazines that one sure sign your kids were on drugs was if their grades started to slip . . . slipped from a 98 on the previous test to a 97 on this test. As if she could tell Andrew Jackson from Andrew Johnson.

The only way I felt I could get her to stop was to show her the real alternative. I simply stopped turning in the assignments. It was a big class, and I knew it would be some time before anyone at the school even noticed. It was my passive-aggressive rebellion, an academic strike. But it wasn't long before Mrs. Thompson, a brusque, direct lady in her late sixties, asked me to stay after class.

She said, "Chris, it's not a big deal. I just want to check in and visit for a while."

I waited around the class as everyone filed out. A couple of kids gave me the side eye, as if to say, *I wonder what kind of trouble he's in.* Given my family circumstances, such concern was not unwarranted.

Mrs. Thompson leaned in to tell me, "Chris, you're failing the class. That is not like you at all. Why?"

I was in a feisty mood. "I just don't care about the grades . . . or, frankly, the material either." She was not buying it. Not any bit of it. She was a wise, experienced educator, a quite sophisticated professional.

"That is a load of equine excrement! [Her proper term for *horses****.] You are one of the smartest kids in the class, and you've never had any trouble mastering the most challenging lessons." She was just getting warmed up. "For whatever reason, you are being lazy and not living up to your potential. But the person you will really disappoint? It's not me. It's not your parents. It's your future self. *That* person will wish he had a time machine so he could go back in time and smack you upside the head!"

The words stung. No teacher had ever spoken so directly to me.

Chagrin. That's what I felt. I'd heard that word, had spelled it correctly, could recognize the definition of it on a multiple-choice quiz. But the truth of it was never so clear.

Chagrin.

I sat there for a moment, alone in my shame. Mrs. Thompson was right.

The silence dragged on for a moment before I blurted out, "You're right. I'm just frustrated, and I can't even tell you all of it. I've never done anything like this before."

We both sat there for another moment, but this time the silence felt easy. We were together in it. I had done the unthinkable and made myself vulnerable, that scared little boy finding the courage to say, "I'm scared."

I asked my teacher my options. "Can I still pass?" My chin was quivering, as much from relief as stress. I was happy to have it out in the open. I took a leap, and Mrs. Thompson's kind eyes told me it was the right choice.

"Well, Chris, if you apply yourself, as I know you are capable of doing, and ace the rest of the assignments, you can still pull your grade up to a C and pass the class," she said.

I had never received a C—ever—let alone failed a class.

I took a deep breath and said, "I will. I'll show you I can do it."

All the way home, my resolve firmed up. I wouldn't let my mother's doubting voice into my head. I would find the time to really do the reading, make notes, pay sharp attention in class, and not space out to stare at Mary Oliver's pretty hair . . . or even to notice the way she smiled at Jack Donovan as if I didn't even exist. I even took up Mrs. Thompson's offer for remedial help to go over the material and study for the tests. It paid off; I virtually aced the rest of the course, earning a hard C. But better yet, I was only one of a very few students in our school who took the national AP History test, passed it, and earned three credits toward my college degree.

When I picked up my report card, with no small amount of trepidation, I was stunned to see that Mrs. Thompson had given me a B minus. I asked her why.

She said, "You earned it. You straightened yourself out and applied yourself. That ability will always serve you well. Life isn't about getting it right all the time. It's about knowing yourself well enough to know what you're capable of, correcting your course, then going out there and doing it . . . and most importantly, not quitting when times get difficult or you feel that you are failing."

Mrs. Thompson had seen through this teen full of self-loathing and anger and had thrown me a lifeline. Her scolding had come at just the right time and was just the right message to reach me. She believed in me.

She woke me up.

CHAPTER 5

Becoming Homeless

LOBSTER HANDS

A mid all the flow of high school life—the sports, hanging out with my friends, the classes, finding myself thinking more and more about girls—the home front was becoming even more turbulent and uncertain. It was 1990 (my senior year was 1990-1991). I was sixteen years old, and there were still six of us siblings living at home, eight family members in all.

My older brother, a cook at a family-style buffet restaurant, had gotten me an interview with the manager, an older man with tired eyes, a bristly mustache, and a shirt pocket full of pens and little notecards. He looked a little like Uncle Rico in *Napoleon Dynamite*. I came prepared, full of sincerity and enthusiasm, and couldn't wait to tell him how I was going to be the most conscientious employee he'd ever had; I would show up on time and do whatever he needed me to do.

The manager shook my hand, looked me over, and said, "You're hired."

It was a hard job, and I guess he figured I could either handle it or I'd quit. It was chaotic: the constant clatter of dishes being bussed into the kitchen; the greasy pile of food to scrape into the trash bin; the scalding hot water blistering my hands; the constant rush of trying to scrape, rinse, and load the industrial-sized dishwasher before the next rush of customers came for lunch or dinner. By the end of the shift, my hands would be red, raw, and sore, feeling more like lobster claws than human. It was the summer before my senior year of high school, and I needed the money to get myself ready for this final year: clothes, sports gear, and even the money I would need to fill out college applications.

It was a busy time, but I've always enjoyed being busy. It left me little time to brood on the everyday sadness of life. But always in the background there was the anxiety at home. How long before we had to pack up and move again? We'd leave behind angry or at least disappointed landlords who felt like schnooks for falling for my parents' sob stories about Mom's "terrible tragedies" and how Dad "is about to land a really important job, and to just give us another month and we'll get it all paid up, and everything will be great." I often remember stacks of unpaid bills that Mom wouldn't even open. The stack would get taller and taller until it would fall over, scattering these urgent letters across the floor like leaves of broken promises.

Eventually the painful nadir of our nomadic life came during the summer after eleventh grade when I was working at the restaurant.

HOMELESSNESS BEGINS

I finished up a shift, enjoying working my first real job (as opposed to the many borderline-legal jobs I had worked at underage) working as a dishwasher at the local restaurant. A coworker was kind enough to give me a ride home that evening. But as we approached my home, I saw the flash of police lights and the very familiar sight of a moving van in front of our home. I don't know to this day if my coworker realized exactly what was going on until later, but I wanted to avoid the embarrassment of his having to drop me off in the middle of the familiar moving drama, so I asked him to drop me off a block or so from the house and thanked him for the ride.

I walked home and saw my parents sitting on the side steps, but I didn't feel any need to ask them what was going on. It had happened so many times before, it was almost routine.

"I'd better help with the packing," I said.

Dad stared at his shoes. "No need for that."

"I'm sorry?"

"The landlord has people packing. They're going to put our stuff in storage."

It took a moment for the impact of that statement to sink in. "Everything? They're putting everything in storage?"

He nodded grimly.

I knew I had to do something. I had no other clothes beyond what I was wearing. I walked to the front door and encountered a police officer and our landlord. Our landlord, a tall, skinny man named Roy, had asked for the police protection so that he wouldn't have to deal with Mom angrily cursing while giving the finger to him or Dad shouting threats at him. Can't say I blamed him. But I felt crushed. My parents had never let on that we had fallen so far behind on our rent . . . again. As I held back my anxiety and developing panic attack, I approached the police officer, terrified of what might happen when I spoke to him.

The police officer seemed sympathetic. "I'm sorry, son."

"Can I at least get inside and get some clothes? I have to go to school. I have to finish school. Do you understand? I have nothing to wear."

The cop looked at the landlord, who was silent for a moment and then nodded. "Go ahead, son," said the police officer.

I went inside and loaded my arms up with a few pairs of pants and a trio of shirts, and grabbed anything else I could for my family. Those items and the clothes I was wearing, grimy with grease and sweat after my shift in the restaurant, would constitute my entire wardrobe.

As I left the house, the cop and the landlord looked away, as though they didn't have the heart to meet my gaze.

I went back to where my parents sat silently and put down the things I had gathered.

"Where are we going now?" I asked.

Neither parent answered. I repeated the question.

Dad finally said, "We don't know. We weren't ready for this. We didn't expect it. We have no plans for another place."

I was stunned. Even for them, even considering the constant uprooting and fleeing debtors and landlords, even through all of that, we had always found another place to live.

"We can't be homeless," I said.

"Well, we aren't homeless, son."

"So do we have somewhere to live or don't we?"

"No," Mom said.

"So we're homeless!"

Now the best we could expect was to shuffle from cheap motel to cheap motel. All of our belongings were loaded on the truck and kept in storage until that unlikely event when my parents could muster up the months of back rent. And I was further crushed when I realized that we would never be able to retrieve those things from storage. The things that had meant so much in our life, that had provided the nearest modicum of continuity for us, the talismans of our lives that showed we had lived—our photos, sports trophies, award certificates, gifts from friends, and other mementoes of our rare happy moments—were gone, forever locked away in some forgotten place.

I had the insight that what mattered most wasn't the clothes, the furniture, or books and tools, but the records of these treasured memories and the people with whom we shared them. They were now forever lost, lost because of my parents' poor choices. It was an abrupt awakening. At that moment, I decided it was also better to lock the vulnerable parts of myself away in a similar forgotten place, never to see the light of day so that I would never face the raw pain of those fragments of myself.

At this moment, Dad stalked around angrily, muttering to himself about the evil world and how it was always out to get him. He then went and hid somewhere until the police left to avoid being arrested.

Mom sobbed hysterically, cursing under her breath, cursing the landlord, God, and everyone she imagined was out to get her. My brothers tried to console her. I walked over to her, this slight woman who was once the darling of her town with her gorgeous honey-colored hair, all draped in curls, framing her pretty face like petals around a rosebud. I looked at her sorry state and was moved with sadness. I felt sad that my parents' poor choices had brought us and them to this point, this precipice from which we had fallen and, I worried, from which we would never rise.

Thus began the most trying of times. On our own. All alone. No direction. No home. No hope. Complete emptiness.

CHAPTER 6

Homeless

We moved into a cheap motel near the freeway, the rumble of trucks the constant backdrop to my sleepless nights, the kind of motel that is featured prominently in horror movies, evoking a sense of dread and foreboding, a place that seemingly has more cockroaches and vermin than guests. We were crammed, all eight of us (ranging in ages from eight to eighteen), into two rooms with two queen beds, sharing one bathroom. I usually slept on the floor. After a week, we moved into an even smaller and cheaper motel.

Dad would clean himself up as best he could, relying on the front office clerk to print out a stack of résumés, and go out to try to secure employment. So far as I could remember, he never held down a job for more than a few months, so it was jarring to see how on his résumé he skipped over many jobs, trying to make it seem as if, by the timeline, he was a steady, reliable employee. I noticed that he listed his sister-in-law, my aunt Meredith, as a reference, as well as other folks, such as his fellow Little League coach, by whom he had never been employed. I hated to see my father made so small and petty with such low-level deceit and trickery. He was a brilliant man with an incredible memory, as he had proven over and over by easily solving the toughest math and calculus problems, or by knowing the answer to any history question before you could even get started.

"Lincoln, on January 1, 1863 —"

"— signed the Emancipation Proclamation!"

"In 1846, when the Mexicans —"

"— crossed the Rio Grande, starting the Mexican–American War. . . . Don't get me started on it . . . not our finest hour, let me tell you."

And so on.

He should have gone on *Jeopardy!* . . . or been able to hold down any of the dozen or so of his menial jobs, such as clerk for a trucking company, or janitor for a warehouse by the freeway, or security guard at the community college. Or maybe that was the problem: the jobs were too menial for a bright, restless mind such as his. Still, there was something broken in him, and my mother too. It wasn't as if the broken pieces came together to make something whole, but rather that they were complicit in each other's dysfunctions. Misery *does* love company.

Misery, Especially with Cats

There was plenty of misery to go around. My little sister loved her cats, two scraggly tabbies she and a friend had found scrounging in a dumpster some months prior. I like cats and have always been kind to animals. Furthermore, animals are often drawn to me, perhaps because of my kind nature. The problem with the cats living with us in the motel room was that more than liking animals, I really liked breathing oxygen.

Unfortunately, I was extremely allergic to the cats' dander, experiencing a severe asthmatic reaction around them. Of course, as if sensing this, they wouldn't leave me alone. If I sat down on the floor or the bed, they'd immediately jump into my lap, mewling for attention. Once, through a backlit window, I could see the floating clouds of their dander, and I started sneezing and wheezing before I even took a breath. It would start with an itchy sensation on the roof of my mouth, spread to my throat, stifling my ability to breathe, and continue until I was practically gasping for air. All my energy would be focused on breathing, but breathing that felt like doing so through a small straw.

Each night, it got to the point that I knew I couldn't sleep if I couldn't breathe, so I'd grab my blanket and pillow and head out to the Chevy truck in the parking lot. It belonged to my older brother, who was back in New York serving as a missionary for two years. This went on for months. Each night, I'd grab my sleeping bag or blankets and head out to the truck, no matter how cold it was, and wrap myself up as warmly as I could and scratch out my homework with a flashlight held in my teeth. Utah, with its mile-high elevations and open, windy plains, can get cold during the winter . . . subzero cold, in fact.

Those nights were interminable. I could never sleep more than a few minutes before the cold would seep into my bones and I would wake up, shivering and shaking. Many nights, the cold and silence were unrelenting. It felt as if the icy hand of death was reaching for me. Sometimes I would brave the cats and dander to go inside the motel room and warm up, until the gasping asthma drove me back into the frozen night. Most nights, the blanket was inadequate protection against the cold, and I would use an old mummy sleeping bag left behind by one of my older brothers, curling up inside it into a fetal position, seeking whatever scrap of warmth I could find. Some nights it was so cold that my hair froze to the metal door.

It seemed there would never be any end to my suffering. No matter how bad it was, though, I would put on a brave face for my classes, for my coworkers, and for my coaches. In fact, I grew especially attached to wrestling practices. I would be the first to arrive at the gym and the last to leave, knowing that the warmth of the gym from the humidity from the sweating bodies would be the last I would feel until the next day.

I felt embarrassed as the coach would often ask, "Chris, is something wrong at home? Do you want to talk about it?"

"No, Coach, it's all good. I just wanted to work on my wrestling moves. I lost last week at the tournament, and I think it's because I'm forgetting the basics. I just need to simplify my form."

"Okay, Chris. You know I'm here if you need me. My office door is always open. But I gotta get home. Hey, my wife is making her famous meatloaf. You want to join us? I'll drop you home after dinner."

Yes, I do! my inner voice practically shouted.

"No thanks, Coach" is what I actually said. "That's very nice of you. But my mom will get worried, and I've got to get on some math homework."

My wrestling coach, Darold Henry, is one of my heroes. He always believed in me and taught me that it was more important to keep trying and not quit, regardless if you won or lost. Then you could sleep peacefully at night, knowing that you had done your best. He also practiced what he preached. School came first for him before sports; he even suspended the team state champion for failing classes. He taught me that school was far more important than sports and had a much longer-lasting impact.

More than once I worried that I had not the strength nor fortitude to deal with the sleeping situation. I so dreaded heading out to the truck, carrying my sleeping bag like a shroud of failure. More than once, the chattering of my teeth woke me up. I would think, *This isn't the worst way to go, actually. Just let the cold win. Let it win, and I will slip away from this vale of tears and find peace. There'd be no one to blame, it would just be an accident. So much better than blasting my head off with a shotgun and leaving a big mess for my family to clean up.*

It all made sense. An easy way out.

CHAPTER 7

Alone

Sometimes at night, I would cry, alone with my tears in the silent darkness. Other times, I would feel angry—angry at the world, angry at my parents, angry at God. Most of the time, I would lie down in the truck, numb from the cold, and try to numb the emotional pain. I'd look up at the startlingly clear sea of stars above, glittering in the cold, clean air. The Milky Way looked for all the world as if someone had taken a bucketful of jewels and strewn the sky with them. It was all so perfect and beautiful up there, so painful and ugly down here.

I wondered many times in those long, cold nights, *Does God exist? And if He does, do I matter to Him?*

It was around this time that my belief in God went from some abstract thing that meant going to church on Sunday and enduring boring sermons and classes to something real and meaningful. I began to understand that these trials and tribulations were a special test and that I could endure, even thrive, as a result of them. If God had sent His Son and allowed Him to suffer, maybe there was something to be learned from suffering. It made me realize that I was meant for bigger things, goals and achievements that I could scarcely dream of, because of these hardships, not despite them. In fact, it gave me an advantage; I was grateful for small things and could struggle through the ordeals that life presented because I knew it was all part of God's plan.

Those cold nights of loneliness and solitude gave me plenty of time to envision that future I wanted, full of promise, beauty, and opportunity.

I would create for my children and family a much better life with the warmth, comforts, and steadiness that I was lacking. I vowed to do better for myself, for them. I couldn't wait to meet them. I vowed that I would learn to endure things I imagined I could not endure. I vowed to become exhausted, striving for those things that were beyond my grasp, never giving up. I knew that I would fail and fall down. I vowed to get back up and keep trying. I knew that I would spend some days and nights with watery, bloodshot eyes, tired from being awake longer than should be humanly possible. But I vowed that I would ultimately become strong, strong enough to reach what seemed beyond my greatest imagining. I vowed to give my future family a life that I had read about and glimpsed in my friends' families. I vowed to make a difference in the world and break the cycle.

Keeping our family fed while living in a motel was a constant struggle. There were lots of sandwiches with cheap deli meats, peanut butter and Wonder bread, and breakfast cereal, sometimes with no milk. It was never enough.

Some days, the only meal I would get would be from my restaurant job. I was grateful that the manager kept me as a dishwasher after school started up in the fall, because they had an all-you-can-eat buffet. I would fill up two, sometimes three plates with mashed potatoes and gravy, mac and cheese, ham, Salisbury steak with mushrooms, bread and butter, and several glasses full of cold whole milk. I was a growing teenage boy "with a hollow leg," as Dad liked to say. Still, after football season ended in November and over the course of three months, I went from a sturdy 180 pounds to a very thin 141 pounds. By February, my jeans began to sag, and I had to notch a new hole in my belt with my pocketknife.

Even more than the all-you-can-eat buffet, my faith nourished me during this dark time. It would not allow me to give up. During my senior year, I worked thirty to forty hours per week at the restaurant and went to school full time. I gave most of my money to my parents to help keep a roof over our heads and help them provide for my younger brothers and sisters. I worked hard at keeping my grades up because I knew that college was my ticket to a better life. I took enough AP courses to earn a large number of credits toward my degree, which meant that in the fall, I would start school as a sophomore. I started varsity football and wrestled as well.

Sports were my sanctuary. Being surrounded by my tight-knit crew of friends, all working toward the same goal, kept me focused and motivated. Even with all this, I participated in student government because I was advised it would look good on my college applications, but also because I felt I had skills that would be valuable for representing the interests of my fellow students. I wondered if my peers ever knew that their senior class officer was homeless. I could trust only a few friends with my secrets.

All throughout that incredibly busy and tumultuous year, I was sustained by my faith in God. I believed that I was a child of God, that I had value and worth despite what the world had given me or what I had been told. This belief gave me the confidence to carry myself proudly despite my situation, to keep my eyes on the future, and to do Him the honor of being grateful for the gift of life.

During these months of living in various motels, we would attend church sporadically, whenever and wherever it happened that we were living at the time, most often in a motel room. I would often go by myself. I would usually sit at the back of the congregation, hoping someone would come to speak to me, to notice me, to acknowledge me, just "see me," as I often felt invisible to the world at this time.

When you are homeless, people try to avoid looking at you, to avoid acknowledging you, to not see that you are a person with feelings and dread. I think it is easier on their consciences that way, lessens their guilty feeling to see their fellow humans living an inhumane existence.

It took a while for all of us to get ready for church. It took special patience for us to be able to use the single-bathroom facilities and get ready, but we were used to it. We took turns staking out our time in the bathroom, occasionally fighting if someone took longer than their allotted time. The bathroom was the one place in the motel room where one could have any privacy and solitude, so that time was a valuable treasure. We became skilled at being efficient in dressing for church and school. What normally takes some kids thirty minutes, we learned to do in less than ten. But by that time, we would be at least somewhat presentable with hair and clothes somewhat improved.

My parents had no money, but they did have pride. No way were they going to let people know that our circumstances truly were desperate. They spent an inordinate amount of effort trying to conceal the chaos in our lives. Instead of focusing that energy on fixing our circumstances, they were more focused on the facade of appearing to have it all together, the facade of a perfect, happy, stable family.

BEING HOMELESS AT CHRISTMAS

When Christmas came around, we were still living in different motels. A few days before Christmas, we had moved to a motel on the foothill bench in Salt Lake City. I always looked forward to Christmas, my favorite holiday. This Christmas I didn't know what kind of holiday we were going to have. The spirit of Christmas was in the air, with music and decorations in the town around us. We didn't have any decorations in the motel and didn't expect to get any kind of presents.

Christmas Eve arrived, and we still didn't have any decorations or presents. That evening we heard a knock on the door. Mom opened it and found a box outside. She brought it in and opened it up.

She called, "Kids, come look! Someone has dropped us off some gifts!"

I went over and looked in the box. There was an assortment of gifts.

Mom said, "Okay, kids, you can pick a gift for Christmas."

I looked in the box and saw a Little Debbie box of Christmas tree snacks. Those looked pretty good to me, so I grabbed them.

That was the only gift I received for Christmas that year.

I opened up the box and had one of the snacks; it was a Christmas-tree-shaped vanilla cake covered with some type of white frosting and candy sprinkles. It was delicious. I had not eaten anything that good for some time. I offered some of the snacks to my siblings, who gratefully accepted. The small gift that some kind person left that year is one of the most memorable I have ever received.

CHAPTER 8

Stumbling Forward

Somehow, I stumbled my way through my senior year, afraid that at any moment I would be exposed as an impostor. I was living a dual life, a lie: a top scholar-athlete; student government leader; a nice, popular kid; hustling and working hard; successful; who had it all together but who in reality was a scarred, broken, sad, lonely shell, a lost child, hoping to freeze to death in my sleep. What was I trying to prove? And to whom? I was exhausted from the effort of maintaining the facade, emotionally drained and physically spent.

Day after day, I worked and suffered and wondered why. Why did I work so hard to maintain this facade? Was it pride? Was it shame? Was it fear?

I believe it was a combination of fear and shame. Fear was my constant companion: fear of the unknown, fear of the world, fear of people. I was also ashamed of the way we lived. I was ashamed that each night, I slept alone in a cold vehicle, alone with my thoughts. Most importantly, I was afraid of what would happen if school authorities or police discovered our circumstances. I lived constantly with the fear of being discovered, that failure to maintain my facade would lead to my siblings being split apart and placed in foster homes. Furthermore, it scared me that my parents would be arrested, and we would never be a family again. I was raised in fear, which was always with me, especially during these dark times, always festering in the back of my mind. When I would lie down at night with only my racing thoughts to keep me company, I imagined worst-case scenarios, strategically developing backup plans to deal with these some-times imagined, sometimes actual catastrophic events.

Looking back, I wish I would have confronted my fear and asked for help from those I had been conditioned to fear. I wish I would have gone to the school leaders, revealed our sad state, and asked for help. Unfortunately, I was taught to fear those who could have helped, those kind souls in the community such as social workers and law enforcement, whose lives are spent trying to rescue others from deplorable conditions. Since that time, I have come to know that it is okay to ask for help, to admit that you can't do everything, and to seek assistance, even from those whom you have been conditioned to fear.

In my lowest moments, oddly, I felt closest to God. I had no one else with whom to share my soul. At night when I was alone, I would speak to God. We were friends having a tough talk, as if He were planning some-thing special for me but wanted to see if I could handle the burdens and responsibilities that awaited me. Plus, church was about the only thing we did as a family. Even if all the other families went out after to Denny's for waffles with lots of syrup and whipped cream, we shambled back to our dingy motel for whatever Mom could scrounge up, usually some bland blend of indigestible glop, usually something lumpy like oatmeal or semi-mashed potatoes.

CHAPTER 9

Conflicting Journeys and, Of Course, Prom

E very day, I made a big journey, from this squalor of the cheap motel to being in the top echelon in our class of four hundred students.

One of the many jobs of student government was planning events. In fact, it was about the only real authority the school administrators would allow us. Every candidate for student council would campaign on the issues. Those who promised to fix the school's lackluster food, get better equipment for the sports teams, or, if they really wanted to flex their muscles, get rid of some of the bad teachers, were the ones who usually won.

It was interesting to me that some of the most popular teachers were the ones who taught the least, who would fire up the VCR and have us watch some old documentary on a semi-relevant subject. And the least popular teachers, the ones the students feared, were the ones who really pushed us to learn, the teachers like Mrs. Thompson, who initially seemed intimidating or remote, even unfriendly, but who were, in reality, the ones who truly cared about us and our futures, truly wanted us to have the tools to succeed in life. As high school students, most of us didn't seem to understand nor appreciate that fact. High schoolers tend to possess a myopic view of the world, focused on themselves at the center.

So even though the students each year would campaign to change the world, the school administrators weren't about to let the students run the show; better to keep us within tight guardrails so that we didn't do anything too stupid.

I decided to run for student government because my friends encouraged me to throw my hat in the ring, and I said, "Sure, why not?"

I ran for senior class secretary. I never actually believed I had any chance of winning because I felt I was not one of the popular kids. I spent my school years keeping my head down, insecure, like most teenagers, which was amplified by my family circumstances. I never let on that school was actually my favorite place in the world, my safe space, the place where I could be truly happy and feel that there was some normalcy in the world. I did not do much to campaign except to stand up and make a speech at a school assembly.

So you can imagine my shock when I won. I believe I won because I was always kind to everyone no matter if they were rich or poor, the smart kid or the kid who struggled. I was even friendly with the kids who dropped out of high school at an early age.

Early in the school year, the student government was summoned to the principal's office. We knew why. It was time to start planning the prom.

The principal, Mr. Lillard, was a friendly man in his fifties, balding on top with a bit of a paunch, but you could tell by the way he moved, smoothly and stealthily, that he had been a standout three-sport athlete in his high school years. In fact, he had coached baseball for years.

He convened the council to go over our responsibilities and time frame for the prom. We spent an hour just choosing the theme. Viva Las Vegas? Too racy. How about London Town? With fog machines and Sherlock Holmes impersonators? Too obscure.

I liked Jenny's imagination. She took her job on the council seriously. A Night in Old Paris, then? Hmm, maybe. Or *The Great Gatsby*? Flapper outfits and tuxedos, art deco decorations?

Someone suggested, "What about A Medieval Night to Remember?"

Now we were heading in the right direction. We decided that we would go for a Victorian renaissance theme and chose the colors magenta and silver. Then we decided on a date. Okay, that important item of business was settled.

Mr. Lillard's voice was soft and whispery, and his eyes darted around the room a lot. His eyes fixed on me. Since I was one of the quieter kids, at times it seemed I might be bored, just going through the motions, and not engaged. In reality, my mind never stops thinking of ideas, including worst-case scenarios and backup plans. I just keep those ideas to myself, not wanting to stand out or fail. But it wasn't Mr. Lillard's first rodeo planning an event. Mine either, but usually my plans involved figuring out where I was going to get food or where I would sleep.

The principal looked at me over his bifocals. "Chris, how much money do you think you'll need this year? I want it to be a first-class event. You guys deserve it."

Everyone's eyes were on me. I stared up at the ceiling for a moment as if I were hoping the answer was written there. I saw the tiles were crumbling and cracked. If he had any budget to speak of, I'd spend it on getting that ceiling fixed if I were him.

"Mr. Lillard, last year's prom budget was tight. I heard they went over budget $200, and people are still complaining about the event. I mean, I heard they did a good job with what they had, but it wasn't everything it could have been. I was not able to attend as I was working." (I actually didn't go because I was working full-time at minimum wage and didn't want to spend my hard-earned money on a dance; I preferred to spend it on food so I could eat.)

Everyone laughed. Even Mr. Lillard. I had never attended any of the dances, I had not asked a girl out at this point, and I felt self-conscious about that. Funny how the best memories are often of the things that felt the worst at the time.

I continued, "I think we need to pick a theme and find a venue. Then we can know the cost and figure out how to raise the money after that."

"Okay, Chris, understood. How much do you think it would take to get the job done, and to do it right?"

The big news from the meeting was always going to be the budget. Students had been pushing for more money for years. Ultimately, though, most of the money for prom—for catering, lights, decorations, advertising, everything—came from the students themselves, from fundraisers and selling tickets. It was a big job. If something, anything, went wrong, we'd get all the blame. If every single thing went right? Everyone would have a great time, but no one would even think to give us any credit. It was like most events: people complain only when it doesn't go well. It is the rare individual who gives praise when things go according to plan. I was okay with that. The responsibility kept me busy and distracted from the turmoil and uncertainty at home, the mindless grind of my restaurant job, and the mental exertion required to keep up my grades on those chilly nights, using the truck's dashboard as my desk.

I had a few thoughts since I had to share. "We should look at the event center at Utah Valley University and see what it costs. If we can afford it, we could hire a real band that can play actual live music, and they'd get the kids dancing. For most dances, everyone stands around like a bunch of zombies, wallflowers, awkwardly waiting for the slow songs so they can dance. We could take out a full-page ad in the school paper. We could get the media arts class to design a proper logo and posters. We could even get Mr. Johnson's theater club to make some castle and other cool medieval decorations. Imagine how fun that'd be to arrive at the gym doors through a castle! Kind of like Cinderella!"

The other kids were just getting warmed up and could feel the energy shifting in the room. Everyone was getting excited.

Johnny asked, "What about finding a local band from Orem or Provo? With cool electric guitars?"

The group concurred. "It would be great to find a real band rather than a DJ."

Other people continued to chime in with various ideas and suggestions. The plan was set. We were off and running.

The next big decision for me was whom to ask. I had quite a few crushes, usually the quiet, nice, studious girls whom I would sit by in class and occasionally try to make awkward conversation with about physics or literature. I was not the most suave or sophisticated smooth talker. (Weren't we all a bit awkward in high school?) Most of them already had boys they were dating. I had never dated in high school as I was afraid and ashamed that the girl would find out about my living circumstances. Dating in high school is difficult for most kids who live a semblance of normalcy, and my peculiar circumstances exponentially amplified that difficulty.

How could I explain to a nice girl, "Oh yeah, we don't have any electricity this month because my parents didn't pay the bill," or "Dinner tonight is tuna fish gravy over tater tots. . . . Mmmm good, let's eat up!" Or that we moved so constantly that she wouldn't find my house, and then I wouldn't be able to call her to tell her the new address. So instead of dating, I just tried to make conversation with girls in class, imagining what it would be like to actually date some of them.

Figuring out who I was going to ask to the dance was extremely stressful. Most of the girls I knew had boyfriends and had already been asked. Each day at school, I looked around my classes, trying to find someone I could ask. Some of my football friends even made a little poster they put up in the hallway, kind of like an Old West wanted poster. It had my picture, then the caption "Wanted: A Date to Prom for Chris Smith." It didn't work but made for some interesting conversations.

As prom got closer and I didn't have a date, I felt panic setting in. I told myself, *How will it look if one of the prom committee members doesn't go to the dance or can't find a date?* I harshly criticized myself. *That would look pretty pathetic.* This was my negative voice in my head from being told I was never good enough, that I would fail. I did not want to fail at getting a date to prom.

Finally, I heard that Julie Stevens had not been asked. I was actually quite shocked. She was one of those attractive girls who could devastate most guys with one glance, one stray smile. And she seemed way out of my league; I was the nice, quiet, smart kid from the strange family who kept to himself. I wasn't one of the popular, cool kids.

Julie Stevens worked with me at the restaurant, where she was everyone's favorite waitress. She knew how to make people feel comfortable, was nice to everyone, and she cleaned up on tips. We had classes together. I didn't think she had a boyfriend, but I knew I'd better move fast. One advantage of being in student government and on the prom planning team was that I knew the date of the prom before anyone else.

Since I was a bit awkwardly shy and since I had never asked a girl out, I opted for a passive option. I bought a bunch of balloons and wrote a note attached to one of them that said, "Julie Stevens, would you do me the honor of attending prom with me? Sincerely, Chris Smith."

It wasn't Shakespeare, for sure, and it wasn't even close to romantic, but it got the message across. One late afternoon, I drove to her house, brought the balloons, took them to her porch, rang the doorbell, and ran off, leaving the balloons to do the hard work of asking her. Let's just say it wasn't one of my shining moments of courage.

Our next shift together, I was closing up for the night. Julie was counting tips and stacking clean aprons. I thought it was a good time to follow up about my invitation.

"Hey, Julie, did you know we'd set a date and theme for the prom?"

"Oh wow, what theme?"

"It is a medieval theme. We're going to get a castle and Renaissance-type decorations, and we're trying to get a real band from Orem or Provo, an actual real band this time..."

"That's awesome, Chris! How exciting!"

"So, I was thinking..." Blood rushed to my face; my ears started burning. "I was thinking, maybe, did you get the balloons I dropped off?" I asked lamely, waiting for her to tell me she already had a date.

She smiled. "Oh yeah, Chris. So what were you thinking exactly?" She was smiling and twirling her hair. She was like a cat with a ball of string.

I smiled too. "Are you going to make me come out and say it?"

She laughed. "Yes, of course I will go to prom with you. I never thought you would ask, and I was worried I would not go to senior prom."

Yes! Success! I shouted to myself.

I went in for a hug, just a brief, friendly hug. I didn't know a girl—anyone, for that matter—could smell so good, like warm sun and baby powder, strawberries with just a trace of lavender.

Pleasant smells aside, I finally had a date for prom!

CHAPTER 10

Dances

GIRLS' CHOICE DANCE

Earlier in the year, before prom time, we had lived in a cheap motel with vibrating beds. Yes, it actually had those stereotypical cheap motel beds from the 1970s (I refused to even sit on that bed, thinking the floor was probably more sanitary). One evening as I came out to the truck to go to bed, I noticed that it was completely covered with hundreds of small paper hearts of every color. I stared, stunned at the truck for a minute, just taking it in.

I asked myself, *Woah, what is this?? A girl actually noticed me?* I found out later that it was Sarah, a nice girl from school who made everyone feel welcome and was a good friend. Then I asked myself, *Wait, how did she find out where I lived?* I had trusted my secret with only a few very close friends on my sports teams. Then I thought, beginning to feel crestfallen, *Ugh. Now everyone will know that I live in a motel.*

I grabbed some of the hearts off the truck and noticed that Sarah had written nice sayings on them such as "You're cute," or "I like you." My heart swelled with emotion as I had been feeling down in a dark place because of my life. Her sweet gesture meant the world to me. It told me that I was not invisible and that I had value. It was the only time that year I was asked out by a girl; in fact, it was the first time I had been asked out by a girl at all. She also kept my secret of where I lived and did not share it around the

CHRISTOPHER L. SMITH, M.D.

school. She had found out about our situation through some of my close friends and wanted to do something to help.

For the girls' choice dance, my friend Robbie Mayo and I met up early at the Purple Turtle for a burger and shake. Robbie and I had become friends working at the buffet restaurant together. He came from a nice family, was a grade below mine, and was one of the humblest, most genuine kids in school. He was a good friend, and my dysfunctional family didn't matter to him. For the dance, I was wearing a nice dark suit that I had found while thumbing through the racks at the Deseret Industries thrift store near the restaurant. It was a little tight in the shoulders when I got it, but hey, it was only three dollars. What I didn't figure was that I was going to lose weight once football was done. It was hard to keep myself fed, and the stress of keeping my grades up and of keeping secrets from my classmates was taking its toll.

So by the time the girls' choice winter dance rolled around, the suit fit perfectly. Robbie and I were both looking sharp. He was over the moon for his date with Millie, and I enjoyed being with Sarah. She was a nice girl, but I was super shy, quiet, and awkward, so I was glad I had Robbie as my wingman to keep the conversation going. It was actually a relief to have the other couple go with us; we both felt like the pressure was off, and we could just hang out and have a good time.

As Robbie and I walked out to the parking lot to go get the girls after eating at the Purple Turtle, we noticed an older lady looking under the hood of her car as if she were staring at hieroglyphics. Thankfully, Robbie was one of the best mechanics I knew; he later opened up a mechanics shop. If anyone could fix the car, he could.

I looked over at Robbie and said, "We should go see if she needs some help."

Robbie quickly responded, "Absolutely! I can probably fix it."

We checked the usual suspects: the distributor cap was fully connected; the battery cables appeared not too corroded. However, when the lady turned the key, the engine just clicked without turning over. The battery was dead. Robbie, as usual, was prepared for any car emergency and fished some battery cables out of the back of his Jeep. He then pulled the Jeep around and jumped the battery to get it to start. Success! We felt good about helping the older lady and didn't accept the money she offered. We felt it was just doing a good turn; Robbie was an Eagle Scout.

We were half an hour late to pick up our dates and not as pristine as we once had been. In fact, both of us had dirty hands from working on the lady's car and smelled of gas. But that was the most event-filled portion of the night. We went to the dance and had a great time. My date with Sarah was a good primer for prom.

THEN TO PROM

Prom night was a long time coming. Julie's parents had insisted months in advance that we take photos in their garden, the low spring sun setting behind the mountains, lighting up our faces with its last rays. I pinned the corsage on her beautiful satin dress, taking care not to poke her. I rode in my friend's car, as my brother Drake's old Blue Chevy truck (AKA my bedroom) was ugly and beat up. My friend had a much nicer car, a Honda! I rented a tux with tails, and I felt rather dashing, if I do say so myself. I had never worn tails before nor dressed so nicely. It was exhilarating.

So, is this what normal kids feel like? I asked myself. It felt great.

When I saw Robbie at the prom, he asked if I remembered jumping that car before the last dance.

"Of course I do," I said. "I would do it again in a heartbeat."

Robbie was one of the best kids I knew, and he would give someone the shirt off his back if he could to help them out. (Who was I kidding? I'm sure I'd do the same thing.) I was happy to see Robbie with Millie at the prom. In fact, they'd been going steady since that earlier dance.

I held Julie's arm as we walked through the castle decorations, whereas only hours before I had been scurrying around with the rest of our prom committee, hanging decorations and helping the crews haul in the dinner and photo booths. The prom committee had really come through for us. That night was one of the highlights of my senior year, a night when I felt I actually belonged. I felt *normal*. I felt *happy*. School and the people in it remained my safe space, my happy place.

CHAPTER 11

High School Graduation

T he kids I grew up with in the Pleasant Grove, Utah area were amazing. Many have gone on to become physicians, attorneys, teachers, CEOs, business leaders, and real estate moguls—most being successful in one way or another. Most importantly, they became like a family to me, a family who believed in me and accepted me for who I was. They were a rare group of individuals. One of the major advantages of being in student government was that I got to hang out with these amazing people, bright and ambitious kids who really cared about making the world a better place.

FRIENDSHIPS AND GRADUATION

Brandon Fugal, my friend since grade school, was the student body president. Other friends from grade school were also involved in student council: Chris Lee from my basketball team and Jason Williams. We formed close bonds through our work and friendship. We also boosted each other's spirits and helped each other study for important tests. Brandon and Chris Lee (Chris 2) had been inseparable since elementary school. Personally, I had a difficult time getting that close to anyone as I felt the need to always protect myself, hiding some of the better parts of me away in order not to be hurt. I envied Brandon and Chris 2 and their friendship; I wished I could have had a friend like that. Yet I still held back, trying to maintain my facade so people would not know I was spending my nights cold and alone in a truck. We formed a good group because we made it a point to be nice to everyone and were as inclusive as high school kids can be.

We all did well on our college placement exams. I scored particularly well on the ACT (American College Testing). The ACT is taken by more than one million students each year, and I scored well into the top one percentile. My scores were one reason I was awarded a full-ride scholarship to the University of Utah. When I received word toward the end of the school year that I was awarded that scholarship, it was a rare, hope-filled moment. I looked forward to the future for the first time in a long time.

Chris 2 also went on to study medicine and become a physician. We all did pretty well on the ACT. But I came in fourth in our class of four hundred students and so was chosen to give a speech at the graduation ceremony. The ceremony was held in front of a packed house at the Brigham Young University basketball arena, the Marriott Center. Since I was also a senior class officer, I was chosen to read aloud the names of each graduating student as they approached the table to accept their diploma.

It was a big day for me, and as I nervously waited backstage, I fidgeted with the three pages of my speech—more than fifteen hundred words that I had spent weeks preparing and rehearsing. To avoid overthinking it, I went through the names of the hundreds of graduating seniors, carefully sounding out each name. Some were tough, tangled with consonants and unfamiliar sounds. We had one student who had transferred from American Samoa: Aea Malomalo Seui. *A-ee-ah Malo-malo Say-wee.* I nailed it.

My speech was titled "Adversity: The Necessary Ingredient for Success." I spoke about people who had overcome adversity: Helen Keller's brilliant mind being shut out from the world because of her blindness and deafness, Benjamin Franklin essentially being kicked out of his home by his father and older brother, Albert Einstein not speaking until he was four years old. History was replete with examples. To use the computer parlance of the day, these weren't bugs; they were features.

When I gave the speech, I looked up from the paper as much as I dared, glancing out at the sea of faces, looking for anyone I recognized. My whole family was there, but I couldn't spot a single one. I chose an older man near the front as my target, making eye contact with him, pretending that we were having a nice, friendly conversation. After the first minute or so,

I settled down. I slowed down my voice, my jokes got laughter, and I felt connected to the audience.

I brought the speech into the current day by talking about the biggest sports star in the world at the time. But first I asked if anyone had heard the name Leroy Jackson. No. Not even a murmur of recognition.

"No? Never heard of Leroy Jackson? Well, Leroy was chosen for the Wilmington, North Carolina, high school varsity squad, and because he was chosen, you know who wasn't? Michael Jordan. MJ. Air Jordan. He got cut. He was relegated to the junior varsity squad and never forgot it. But instead of whining about how unfair life was, he used that rejection as fuel, fuel to overcome the doubters and the haters, the people who never gave him a chance. He told ESPN, 'Whenever I was working out and got tired and figured I ought to stop, I'd close my eyes and see that list in the locker room without my name on it.'

"That's what it looks like to overcome adversity: not complaining about it, but using it as motivation to do great things.

"Furthermore, part of overcoming adversity is giving back, devoting ourselves to service and the betterment of mankind, honoring the sacrifices of those who came before us to make the world a better place. Nothing would be more dishonorable and insulting to those brave men and women than our apathy."

I got a standing ovation.

Had I to do it all over again, I would have talked about my own adversity, my own struggle. Only a few friends knew that I was homeless throughout that year. Sharing that would have allowed sunshine in to help heal those wounds, to let people know that I was having a hard time and that a kind word of encouragement every now and then would have made a world of difference. I had worked so hard to keep things under wraps that a shadow followed me everywhere, taunting me, making me feel exposed and vulnerable. I had heard that Catholics confess their sins because then the devil can't use those sins against them. I felt a little like that, as though my shame was being used against me, except not by anyone else but by me myself, the voice in my head that constantly told me that I was not good enough, the fear that I would fail.

The whole ceremony left me feeling good about myself, confident, and ready to shoulder the burdens of the future.

Little did I know that the worst was yet to come.

TROUBLE AHEAD

I got a hint earlier in that school year about what was to come. One afternoon towards the end of my senior year, I was waiting for my parents to pick me up after classes. I had the night off from the restaurant and was looking forward to studying for my Physics AP test. A lot hinged on my getting a good score, and I felt weak on the optical physics portion of the test. The math I knew backward and forwards. The science was second nature. But we reviewed prep questions in our AP Physics class, and all of us failed. I was not going to blow an important chance to transcend my circumstances and make something of myself. I vowed to not fail.

I sat waiting at the bottom of the hill by the school sign on a boulder where I often sat, the sun warm on my face, listening to my Walkman. It was my only possession, my prized possession, and I never went anywhere without it. I learned early on in my life that most things go better with music, and certainly that was the case with waiting. I did a lot of waiting. My parents were always running late. Why, though, I never understood. My father didn't have a job at the time. In fact, I was the only one of us still living with the family who had a job. Usually, they were thirty-five to forty minutes late, like a consistently slow clock, but this time the minutes stretched into an hour.

I played both sides of my favorite cassettes, Air Supply's *Live in Hawaii* and Guns N' Roses' *Appetite for Destruction*. It'd be hard to find two bands more different—one with poppy love ballads and the other gritty and hard, though I must admit "Sweet Child of Mine" was a great tender ballad. Guns N' Roses' music sounded like it was written for me. "Welcome to the Jungle" could have been describing my life:

> Welcome to the jungle, it gets worse here every day
> You learn to live like an animal in the jungle where we play
> If you got hunger for what you see you'll take it eventually
> You can have anything you want but you better not take it from me

I knew Axl Rose was a terrible role model: self-destructive and nihilistic. But I wished I had his freedom to just tell it like it was and not the happy fantasies we tell ourselves to get by. And Slash's guitar playing?

That was a different matter—he was polished and confident because he practiced all the time. Discipline. I guess there was something in Guns N' Roses to appeal to both sides of my nature.

Air Supply, on the other hand, was pure guilty pleasure. I can imagine the teasing I would have taken if any of my friends had found out. It might as well have been ABBA (though I did like ABBA too). "I Can Wait Forever" was one of my favorite songs from *Ghostbusters*, one of my favorite movies. And "All Out of Love" soothed me on those all-too-frequent occasions when I had heartache. Plus, it reminded me of my older sister Darlene and happier times with her.

Finally, both Mom and Dad showed up. Instead of taking a left to head out to our motel just off the highway, we headed in the other direction, to the Ford dealership. I was mystified. My dad stalked around the lot with a salesman, literally kicking tires, listening to the sound of a door swinging shut.

"Hear that, son? That solid *thunk*? That's good old-fashioned American craftsmanship. Not like those Chryslers, for goodness' sake."

The salesman looked the part: short-sleeved shirt, too-short tie that curled up at the end, thinning hair combed over his bald spot. He looked like a man who had either made a lot of bad choices or had had a lot of hard luck. Truth was, probably some of both. I couldn't understand why in the world we were wasting our time, and his. We couldn't afford a roof over our heads let alone a car, not even the most rusted-out jalopy on the back lot.

I put on my headphones, and "Crazy Train" by Ozzy Osbourne was playing.

> . . . *Mental wounds not healing. Life's a bitter shame. Going off the rails on the crazy train.*

It seemed to be a perfect accompaniment for the surreal moment I was experiencing, as if I had been transported to some twilight zone alternative reality.

Mom acted all officious as I'd seen her do, usually when people expected her to pay them what she owed. "And no, don't even ask," she said. "We will not be taking out an extended warranty. If the car breaks down in the first six months, Utah just passed a lemon law, and you are bound to give us our money back."

The salesman said little but riffled through a pile of papers, carefully turning the documents around so they faced my parents, who pored over them as if they were about to sign.

Mom said, "This here? Is that the best interest rate you have? That seems a lot higher than the Toyota lot down the street."

Dad chimed in. "They were offering 8 percent with only 10 percent down. You're expecting 10 percent with 15 percent down. It doesn't add up."

The salesman said, "Well, if your credit is as good as you say, then we'll have no problem making better terms. These are just the introductory offers."

I winced. No way my parents had any credit, let alone good credit.

I put the earphones back on and listened to "Paradise City."

> Just an urchin livin' under the street
> I'm a hard case that's tough to beat
> I'm your charity case so buy me something to eat
> I'll pay you at another time
> Take it to the end of the line

Paradise City? Yes, that was ironic, and I felt as if I were living the irony they were singing. No paradise for me, stuck in this weird Kabuki theater with my parents, watching them waste this poor man's time.

Finally, we left the dealership just as the staff was closing up. Mom and Dad huddled up with the salesman.

"We'll be back with the down payment tomorrow. Please hold that Taurus for us," Dad said.

I hoped the salesman wasn't going to go out and spend that commission. I knew he was never going to get it.

"Mom, what was that all about?"

Mom and Dad looked over at each other. She sighed. "There was a misunderstanding about the rent we owed at the motel. The manager told us he'd comp us for several nights because the electric switch plate was broken, and oh boy, if one of the kids got shocked, he'd have a heckuva lawsuit on his hands."

Dad nodded. "I told him not once but three times. It took him two days to send someone over. He can't expect us to pay for those days when we were in danger!"

Mom continued. "That awful man locked us out of the room, and we couldn't get our stuff. So we're just killing time until they finish. Hopefully they'll let us keep a few things. Can you believe these people?"

I thought, *What people, Mom? People who expect to get paid the money that's owed them?*" I said nothing and put my headphones back on. Here we go again...

Going off the rails on the crazy train...

CHAPTER 12

Family Falling Apart

A few months later that summer, I was seventeen years old, and we were still living in a motel, this time in the Motel 6 in Provo, Utah. This was shortly after my senior year had ended and I'd graduated from high school. One afternoon as I walked into the restaurant to start my shift, I smelled fresh-baked bread, scones, and roast beef. I thought, *This is going to be a great day. What is better than the smell of fresh bread?* I clocked in, put on my maroon apron, tied my strings, straightened my tie, and got ready for work.

Work at the restaurant consisted of cooking food and putting it out buffet style. Most of the food was actually fresh and not frozen. We would cook a variety of foods, from fresh-baked scones to fresh-baked bread, roast beef, dressing, and corn, typical western-type food. Each night the restaurant would have a special item; for example, Thursday was Italian night. The day before, I would make all the lasagna for the entire night from scratch, with fresh-made noodles, sauce, and meat. I would spend at least four hours prepping the lasagna. For each, I would place a roll of noodles on the bottom, sauce and cheese, and then noodles, and eventually create a lasagna with the sprinkled cheese on top.

This night as I went to work, I was feeling some hope for the future. I had graduated high school, and I had that four-year scholarship to the University of Utah. I began work by cooking food to put out on the line. Evenings and nights like these were quite busy, with work being nonstop action at the restaurant. Many people liked to eat there and spend time together with their families.

On this night, I remember I was working very busily when the assistant manager, Tom, said, "Chris, you have a call." I was a bit confused as I never received any calls. I left the kitchen and picked up the phone, and I heard my little brother, who was ten years old at the time, crying and distraught. He sobbed, voice cracking, "The police came and arrested Dad, and he is going to jail. Mom has gone crazy and is going to kill herself and jump off a bridge."

I stood for a moment as if I had been slapped breathless, momentarily paralyzed and in shock. This seemingly came out of nowhere (though in reality, events had been slowly building for years leading to this outcome). I felt completely overwhelmed and was at a loss as to what to say next.

How do you respond to something like that? When you are told that your parent is going to kill themselves and you have only mere seconds to change the outcome? This situation was well beyond my ability to handle at seventeen years old.

I quickly snapped back to reality, trained by my years of anxiously imagined worst-case scenarios. I quickly told my brother Tom, "Hurry. Hang up and go follow Mom because if you are with her, I don't think she will kill herself. Hurry! Run!" I almost screamed it into the phone.

He said, "Okay," hurriedly hung up the phone, and went to follow Mom to prevent her from committing suicide. (I later learned that quick decision may have saved her life. I found out that the only reason she did not kill herself was that Tom had followed her, and she could not bring herself to do it in front of him.)

Shell-shocked, I slowly returned to work as food needed to be made and I needed to be paid, even more so now. I did not tell my boss what was going on and tried my best to hold up the facade. Externally I was hiding it pretty well and did my job. Internally I was a mess of emotions, like a washing machine on an uncontrolled spin cycle, my head spinning about solutions. I worked the rest of my shift for the next two hours, worried sick about what was going on with my parents and siblings, not knowing what was going to happen but imagining the worst.

When I finished my shift, I got a ride back home to the motel. When I arrived, there were sirens and law enforcement personnel outside, a scene that seemed surreal but all too familiar. I walked over to where everything was going on and saw my older sister. She was with my younger siblings. I kindly asked one of the police officers if I could go into the motel room and get the money that I had earned and given to my parents to provide for my siblings. It was the only money I had in the world, maybe thirty or forty dollars. I desperately needed it to be able to eat or drive. When we lived in the motel, I would give nearly all the money I made to my parents so they could get food and other things for my younger siblings

I looked around. Mom was not there, and I grew concerned about her. Dad was not around either. I asked Darlene where our parents were. She said Dad had been arrested and taken to jail—I never learned why—and Mom had been taken to a psychiatric unit because she was planning on harming herself. I was at a loss. All the hope that I had been feeling earlier that day was quashed in an instant, and I had no idea what to do.

I went into the motel room and grabbed a few of my belongings, a couple of shirts and a couple of pairs of pants so I could change out of my work clothes. We stayed the night at my older brother Darwin's house. Eleven years older than I, Darwin had been married for some years now and had a couple of children. I lay there trying to sleep, numb inside and broken. Any stability I'd had was now gone. I felt alone and empty but grateful for my siblings. I eventually fell asleep, shell-shocked, not knowing what was going to happen, if we were going to be taken into custody by the state. I was in that in-between stage because I was still a minor but had already graduated from high school.

CHAPTER 13

Alone, Finding My Own Path

The next morning, my brother and I discussed what we should do to handle this latest crisis.

Darwin said, "I visited Dad in jail [I still don't know why Dad was in jail], and it was just like the movies, with him in an orange jumpsuit." Darwin began to tear up and continued, "I even had to go through a security checkpoint in order to see him. It was pretty shocking to see him like that. Dad is pretty upset and embarrassed. He is worried about us, his kids, and Mom." He said he didn't know what was going to happen as far as charges or jail time.

Darlene said, "Mom is pretty messed up right now. She is still in the lockdown psychiatric unit of the hospital, and they aren't sure when she is going to get out because she is not in a good place mentally or emotionally. She still wants to kill herself." We continued to counsel each other to try to figure out what to do.

We decided that my younger siblings would be split amongst my older siblings and my aunts and uncles as we tried to find a place for us to live until my parents got out. As we were separating, we did not know what the future was going to bring, and it was a sad time. Some of us cried at the meeting. It was decided that I was going to go stay briefly with my aunt and uncle about an hour and a half away. I drove up there by myself so I could stay the night with them as I did not have anywhere else to go. On the way, I felt quite lonely and abandoned, alone in the world and without direction. Any ounce of hope that I had felt previously was gone. I did not know what to do. The next day, I drove back to the motel after work to pick up whatever items I could, hoping to get a few more clothes.

When I arrived, I found out that Mom had been released from the psychiatric hospital and had decided to immediately leave the area and go to Idaho to live with her sister. She felt that was the only place she could stay until she figured out something. She had abruptly left before I arrived at the motel, taking my younger siblings with her. I was left in Utah as I had graduated, and I was an "adult" even though I was only seventeen years old. I didn't even get a chance to tell them goodbye, just as with all the friends I had lost over the years from all of our constant moves.

I also learned that Dad was going to spend at least a month in jail, and we did not know exactly when he was going to get out. I never did get a straight story as to what the actual charges were or why he was in jail. I just know he spent at least a month or more in jail. I never spoke to him about it or what it was like for him to be there.

Some weeks later, Mom showed up at my aunt and uncle's house where I was staying and asked me to go to Idaho to help her take care of my siblings. I was at a crossroads at this point because I had my scholarship to the university, which I felt was going to pave the way to a better life. Mom didn't really care about that. She just felt desperate and wanted to find a way out of her situation and make a better life. She wanted me to help provide for her and help her as I always had.

I decided at that point that I needed to go out on my own, that my parents and their problems were way above my ability to fix, and that I needed to go to school to create a better life for myself. School was always the stable influence in my life, one of the few things I could count on to be consistent. School was by far more stable than my parents and family, and it truly had been one of the few places I had been happy in my life. It was the one place where I could thrive despite my background or what was going on in my life.

I said, "Mom, I can't fix your problems. I can't be the one to provide for you. I am sorry, but you are going to have to figure it out yourself."

When she left me at that time, Mom told me, "Well, I love you. I wish you were coming with us." She did not give me a hug or anything, then said she would see me some time. She always had difficulty expressing physical affection. I suspect it might have been from the way she was raised.

After that, I was on my own. I was an adult even though I was only seventeen. I needed to make a plan. So I called my older sister, who lived closer to my work, and asked her if I could stay with her and sleep on the couch. I didn't have anywhere else to go. She agreed. I will always be indebted to her because she saved me, both physically and emotionally. Without her, I would have been completely lost.

I now had what many teenagers at age seventeen only dream of: *complete freedom*. No one to tell me what to do, where to go, or when to come home. No one to tell me how to dress or what I should do with my life. Yet with that freedom, I also had complete responsibility for myself. I also was alone. It is hard for me to describe the complete emptiness and abandonment I felt. Prior to this, despite everything else going on, I had always had my siblings to lean on. They were now gone except for my older sister, whom I saw as a knight in shining armor who had saved me.

CHAPTER 14

College!

FIRST YEAR OF COLLEGE

As I began my first year of college, I was at the ripe old age of seventeen. I lived with Darlene, over an hour away from the college. I would sleep on her couch every night and each day had a very similar routine.

In the morning, I would get up by 5:30 a.m., walk about a mile to catch the bus at 6:00 a.m., and ride over an hour to the college, changing buses a couple of times. Some mornings were cold, others not too bad. On the ride, I would try to either catch up on my sleep or study. Each day I would try to make my first class, calculus, by 7:30 a.m. I really regretted taking calculus first thing in the morning; thinking about complex math at 7:30 a.m. was really a chore. Then I would stay at the college and study in between my classes, eat lunch at midday, and then take the bus home at approximately two or three o'clock in the afternoon. I would then walk approximately a mile and a half to work to start my shift by four o'clock.

My work shift consisted of either cooking and prepping food, or washing pots, pans, and dishes for at least six hours until ten o'clock at night. Then we would clean up for about an hour afterward in order to go home. Most weeks I would work Monday through Saturday, sometimes even Sunday. Add that to five days of school a week and it made for a compressed and hectic life.

My first year in college, I took seventeen credit hours each semester. I had calculus, chemistry, biology, and chemistry lab, and each semester,

I also tried to take a "fun" class. My first semester, I took bowling, which was my recreation for the first year. Every Tuesday and Thursday, we would practice bowling for an hour or so. The test consisted of scoring properly. By the end of the semester, I actually got to be decent at bowling. The second semester, I did weightlifting and softball as my fun classes. Coed softball was quite fun, and I enjoyed weightlifting and exercise.

My other classes were pretty intense. Most of the time I would study at the student union or the library. At this time, Nirvana had hit the scene. "Smells Like Teen Spirit" was on all the TVs, and people watched MTV while they tried to study. I would try to find a quiet little nook in the student union or a quiet corner in the library. I didn't talk much with people because I usually didn't have time; I tried to maximize my free time by studying as much as possible. I did have a few friends I would occasionally study with. Usually, they wanted me to help them study more than helping me study; once people in the classes found out I did well in school, they would try to become a "study buddy" with me.

Similar to my younger years, the library was my safe haven. I frequented the University of Utah library as often as I could. And when I had a rare day off, I would put on my Walkman and backpack, and walk the three miles from my sister's house to the Orem city library. Talking and singing to myself, I happily strode to the library with anticipation, as if I were meeting some old friends for dinner, old friends such as Gandalf and other literary characters. After I arrived, I would spend several hours there, browsing, reading, just breathing in the peaceful ambiance of the library. When I was done, I would check out some books, then walk the three miles back home. I didn't do much else for fun, but when I was in the library and found a good book to read, I had all the entertainment I needed. I feel that reading, learning about the world, and developing your imagination is a critical element of becoming successful in any field. Books hold enormous power to inspire, to give hope and capacity to overcome adversity.

BUNGEE JUMPING

I did not have much of a social life during my freshman year as I was always working and studying. I never joined a fraternity and never went to many parties, but every now and then, I did something impulsive. I was driving home from work one day and saw a crane at the local college that had a small basket on top. The crane would take people up, who would then bungee jump out of the bucket. The crane was around 125 feet tall. I randomly decided that I would go bungee jumping. I figured, *Why not? I may as well try it.*

After I rode the crane basket to the top and looked down 125 feet below me with nothing but air and the ground, I started to second-guess my spontaneous decision. The people below looked as small as ants. I screamed inside, *I don't really want to do this!* But I figured I had gone all the way up there, so all I could do was go for it. I didn't want to have the "ride of shame" down in the basket reserved for those who couldn't jump.

I leaned forward over the edge of the basket, looked straight down at the people, took a few quick breaths, and told myself, *Okay, you got this.*

Then I let go.

Gravity. Gravity took its unforgiving effect. I plummeted straight toward the ground, accelerating at thirty-two feet per second, not able to breathe as the wind whipped past. I looked at the ground as people rapidly got larger, and the ground loomed like a terrible ending as I fell headfirst toward it. I felt as if I were going to die, making a large-splatter mess of blood and body parts on the ground. I screamed at myself all the way down, "*What were you thinking? Idiot! That was stupid! AAAGGGHHH!*" My life flashed before my eyes as time slowed to a crawl.

Suddenly, a few feet before I hit the ground, the bungee cord snapped back and pulled me airborne again. I felt as if I were floating in the air like a fluffy white cloud in the summer meandering across the sky. It was one of the coolest feelings *ever* . . . such a contrast to the fear of a terrible death I had felt moments before. The feeling was intoxicating, a delicious cocktail of adrenaline surging throughout my body.

I proceeded to gently bounce up and down a few times until I slowly descended to the ground. When I landed, my heart was beating outside my chest, and my body felt as if it were ready to explode. My arms and legs were shaking and tingling from the serious adrenaline rush.

I learned from this experience that sometimes the only way to proceed forward is to lean over the edge and let go, trusting in those things and people who support you. Even though you're afraid, you can still leap and let go. You may fall or fail, but eventually you will bounce back and feel as if you are on a cloud as you rise back up. Afterward, it will feel that it was a great experience, that you learned a lot about who you are inside, and that you were able to conquer your fears to accomplish something.

My Low Point

At the end of my freshman year of college, I had earned enough credits to be nearly through my sophomore year because of my rigorous schedule and my Advanced Placement classes. However, because I was working so much and going to school, I was not able to maintain a high enough GPA, which was a 3.5 requirement, to keep my scholarship. I ended up with a 3.45 GPA for my freshman year; 0.05, a minuscule *fraction* of a percent, but one that made all the difference; 0.05 . . . the small semblance of order that I had created that year was gone; 0.05 can change the world, both for better or for worse; 0.05 . . . I lost my scholarship, and the world caved in on me, again, like a landslide. I didn't know what to do. No direction. No future. *Nothing.* All lost because of that 0.05.

After I lost my scholarship, I had worked so hard for my entire life, even working hard during the motel days, I became severely depressed, completely directionless. I felt as if I had lost any chance of success in life. I felt as if I had lost the plan I had made to create a life for myself and my future family, and any chance for a better life was gone. I became very negative and hard on myself and was in a dark place. I didn't even feel like waking up to try to live. I felt like a complete failure. I was afraid that I would end up working in the restaurant industry for the rest of my life; there's nothing wrong with that, but I wanted a better life and did not want to wash dishes and cook for low wages and not use the talents with which I had been blessed. I didn't know what to do. I was lost, lost in myself, trapped in the misery of my mind.

CHAPTER 15

Quitting and Beginning Again

U p to this point in my life, I had never used alcohol or drugs of any kind or even smoked cigarettes. I was in a dark place, down on myself and so depressed, hurting so bad inside that I felt torn apart and crushed, my reserve gone. I was completely lost, alone, and abandoned, without hope or direction. I felt the old familiar darkness closing in on me again, that my soul was fractured and crushed to the point that I was going to quit.

A searing pain filled my heart and mind; I just didn't want to go on. Each day, even though the sun would rise, inside the darkness grew darker and darker as I became sadder and sadder, seeing myself as a failure, telling myself that I was a failure. I completely lost my desire to try to pick myself up.

One night at work, I decided that I needed to numb this burning pain in my soul. I made the poor decision to try to numb it with alcohol. I convinced one of my coworkers who was of legal age to buy us some beer, wine, and other spirits so we could get drunk and I could forget the deep sorrow and pain in my heart. We bought the booze, and four of us went to her family's house because they were not home. We started to play some drinking games such as beer pong and took shots. The night passed quickly and rapidly became a blur as nights like this often do. I remember the numbing sensation washing through my soul as I no longer felt pain or cared about the future anymore. I didn't care about much. I remember falling over and passing out at some point.

The next morning, I woke up with a massive headache, and I felt terrible physically and mentally. I had the physical pain of a merciless hangover. I felt sick and nauseated, had a headache, and felt like a freight train was in my head.

More importantly, the pain in my heart and soul was still there, but it had grown, amplified to an even larger darkness, an abyss, because in addition to the feeling of emptiness and loneliness, I knew I had also *betrayed* myself by discarding my core values. I had quit, giving up on myself and everything I held precious. I had *failed*. I had *failed* because I had *quit*.

We never truly fail as long as we keep trying.

But this time, I had quit and given up. It was all on me; I couldn't blame my parents or anyone else for what I had done. At some point, we become accountable for our own choices and, consequently, our own outcomes. It was my choice, and because I chose to quit, the failure was *all on me: my choice, my failure*.

However, the good thing about failure is that failure is not final. It is not the end. We can choose to learn from failure, to change the next outcome. We have an amazing depth to change, to grow, I would even say metamorphize and reach heights we never even dreamed of. This realization crept over me, and I decided self-deprecation, self-medication, and wallowing in the tragedy of the past was not the way I wanted to live my life. I did not want to become a person who numbed his pain with substances and made things only worse by doing so.

I didn't want to end up in an even darker hole, an alcoholic who had wasted those talents I had been given, so I decided that I needed to do something differently, to not let the tragedy of my childhood become the recurring nightmare defining the rest of my life, a type of double tragedy wherein one tragedy defines us and we let it ruin the rest of our lives, not moving on and wallowing in the sludge of the past. I like to think of this analogy: If someone walks by and punches us in the face, do we continue to punch ourselves in the face every time we see that person, never moving on and letting that person or their behavior own us for the rest of our lives? Or do we move forward, choosing our own path so that they can never hit us in the face again?

I thought about a variety of possibilities, including joining the military, going back to college, working in the restaurant, or just throwing in the towel completely and ending my life.

At that moment, I felt that there was a voice in my head telling me, *I need to lose myself in helping others. I need to stop focusing on myself and start to help others, and doing so will help to heal my fractured heart.*

CHOOSING SERVICE TO OTHERS

I decided that I would choose my future, create my future. I would let my failure be only a temporary learning experience, leaving it as one more scar I had earned in my life. I decided that at the least, I could choose to work hard, and at the end of the day, no matter what happened in the future, I could tell myself that I didn't quit.

For the next six months or so, I worked very hard for fifty to sixty hours a week and saved the money in order to leave and volunteer my service to others somewhere else. During this time, the longest stretch I worked was fifty days straight without a day off.

Ultimately, I saved a decent sum of money and decided to go do missionary and community service work. I was called by my church to serve in Southern California. I ended up in the inner cities and barrios of Orange County, California, primarily in Anaheim, Santa Ana, Garden Grove, and Westminster. I learned Spanish so I could communicate with the population that resided there.

CHAPTER 16

Mission: Missionary Work

I n order to become a missionary, I attended the Missionary Training Center in Provo, Utah for nine weeks. This was an intensive training program in which we studied for over twelve hours a day, learning the basics of Spanish and how to teach lessons on the Gospel of Jesus Christ. After nine weeks, we were sent to our missions in various places around the world.

My first day in the mission was eventful.

My trainer, Elder Matthews (every male missionary of The Church of Jesus Christ of Latter-day Saints is referred to as an Elder), picked me up from the airport and said, "Let's get to work and go knock on some doors, Elder." He didn't even let me unpack or change my clothes. We promptly left, knocked on doors for many hours that day (all day and evening), and then finally went to our apartment to rest at 9:00 p.m.

Speaking Spanish meant I would often be in some of the rough areas of SoCal. There are many gangs in SoCal, especially in the poorer neighborhoods. I was often similar in age to the gang members. I enjoyed teaching gang members, trying to tell them about God, and trying to get them to see the world differently. I genuinely liked most of the gang members, and I thought most of them were just like me; they had simply made a few different choices. Most of the gang members had been raised in the religion of their parents, which happened to be Catholic. Because of that, they respected religious teachers and treated us gracefully.

TEACHING GANG MEMBERS ABOUT GOD

One day, my companion and I were walking along in a pretty rough neighborhood. Both of us stood out quite dramatically as we walked along in our white shirts and ties with our black name tags on. People could clearly identify us as missionaries. As we walked, we saw a group of gang members arguing on the corner. The argument was quite heated, and they seemed as if they would break into a knife fight or shoot-out at any moment. We honestly did not know if they were carrying guns or knives and were about to throw down in a brawl.

My companion and I looked at each other and said, "Let's go."

We didn't hesitate and walked right into the middle of the group to separate them.

I warmly told them, "*Buenas tardes.* Do you believe in God? Do you want to learn more about God?"

Both of the groups stared at us as if we were from another planet, but their anger at each other quickly disappeared and was replaced by confusion from our unexpected appearance. The leader of one of the gangs, fearsome looking, muscular, tattooed, with a shaved head, and who was dressed in the white tank tops and saggy jeans favored by some gang members, spoke up. He told us, "Hey, man, where are you from? You ain't from around here. You ain't from this barrio."

We said, "Utah."

He said, "Oh, you're those weird Mormon dudes," genuinely laughing as he said it. I preferred his laugh over other less desirable responses.

I said, "Yeah. We are missionaries sent from God and would like to tell you about Him."

He continued, "So what do you want to tell us about God? What does He want us to know?"

I said, "We are all children of God, and we are all brothers and sisters, and God loves all of us."

He further continued, "Hey, man, that's cool. Right on." Motioning to his gang, he said, "We believe in God. We are Catholic, man. My *abuelita* used to drag me to mass."

We said, "That's great. You are Catholic, so you believe in Christ."

He said, "Yeah, man. Straight up!" Some others also began to chime in that they used to go to mass.

I said, "That's great. Do any of you want to come to church with us and see what we are like?"

At that point, this fearsome-looking tattooed gang leader said, "Man, you guys are alright and pretty cool. You seem like some pretty cool dudes. Anytime you want to come tell us about God or be in our neighborhood, that is cool with us."

He shook our hands, and then his gang slowly retreated, laughing and joking amongst themselves.

Shortly thereafter, we were knocking on doors in the neighborhood, and we ran into a fifteen-year-old kid who was part of the gang. His name was Victor. He was a little shorter than us, had a kind of cherubic face with a shaved head, and was wearing a white tank top with saggy jeans.

He opened the door with a huge smile and said, "Come on in. I saw you guys the other day when you told us about God."

We went in, and we talked to him about God. We told him, "God lives and loves you." We also told him, "You know you have value. You can do more than be in a gang. You could even go to college, maybe even become a doctor or a lawyer."

We met with Victor for a couple of months, and he began to attend church. He started to hang out with the kids who were in the youth group at church and stopped hanging out with his gang member friends. He went back to school and was planning on going to college. The idea that he had value grabbed hold of his mind and became a strength for him to change his life.

I left the area shortly after that, so I never heard what happened to Victor, but he was determined to make a better life for himself. I sincerely hope he did.

Victor was important to me as he taught me that I should not judge people because of their appearance or what they may be involved in. Everyone has potential. It showed me that there are good people who just make some bad choices or who grow up in environments where they don't know anything different, that once they are given a chance, they can change and become something better.

STRANGERS CAN PROVIDE UNEXPECTED KINDNESS

A few months later, on a beautiful summer day, we were walking in another rough neighborhood when we noticed a police squad car driving past, which then whipped rapidly around in the street and pulled slowly up to the curb next to us. My heart began to race as panic set in; I could hardly breathe, feeling anxiety exploding inside me because I had been conditioned to fear police my entire life. The police officer slowly rolled down his window. I saw he was a large, strong, burly man with a crew cut, wearing dark sunglasses and a bulletproof vest. He had that intimidating demeanor that law enforcement personnel develop after years of working in the field.

The officer called over to us with his brusque, commanding voice, "Hey, you guys, come over here. I need to talk to you."

I felt panic skyrocket in my brain. I glanced at my companion, perplexed, wondering if we had done something wrong. It did not seem that we had done anything wrong as we were just minding our own business, strolling along the sidewalk, enjoying the sunny day. But we made our way slowly over to the car window.

The police officer leaned out the window and said, "Hey, you look like nice kids. Do you know what kind of neighborhood you're walking around in?"

I said, "Yeah, it's a bit rough, but we are just missionaries walking around trying to talk to people."

He then said, "Hey, I'm worried about you kids being in this area. I need to warn you that this is a really rough neighborhood." He proceeded to tell us, "Look, even as a police officer, I don't feel comfortable being in this area. It is a bad, bad neighborhood. I only come in here armed, in my squad car, and wearing a bulletproof vest."

Relieved, I said, "Thank you so much for looking out for us, but we walk around here all the time. We should be okay as missionaries."

He looked at us, taken aback, and, somewhat incredulously, said, "Okay, suit yourselves, but be careful. Watch yourselves. I don't want anything to happen to you kids." And he drove away.

I was stunned as I watched him drive away. All of my life, I had been taught that police were the bad guys who couldn't be trusted and were not good people. This kind man's actions taught me more of actual reality in one moment than all the years of falsehoods with which I had been indoctrinated as a kid. I realized that police officers can also be good people. This complete stranger had taken the time to look out for us and to try to help us.

At this moment, I began to understand, as my myopic worldview was expanded, that even people who are strangers can be good to us and do nice things. There are many good people in the world who try to live their lives as best they can by doing small acts of good in the world.

Most of my life, I had been taught to fear people because they were out to get you, that I couldn't trust anyone, that I needed to always have a wall built around me for protection. I was also incorrectly taught to especially fear police officers because they are the enemy, always out to get you. However, this man's actions showed me that my beliefs were actually incorrect and that I needed to see the world and needed to see people with a more positive perspective.

But Not Everyone Is So Nice

A few months later, we were walking down the street on a nice sunny California afternoon. Out of nowhere, a loud sound shattered the quiet afternoon as a small silver Honda turned around the corner quickly, tires squealing, and then rapidly slowed. We were startled.

At that moment, a man leaned out the car window and started shooting at a house about fifty feet away from us, peppering it with bullets. *Bang! Bang! Bang!* He loudly shot at the house.

Terrified, we dove behind a car, not wanting to become collateral damage. The Honda then burned its tires as it quickly drove off in the other direction.

Shortly thereafter, I drove a mission car to pick up some other missionaries to take them to another location. We knocked on the door of their small apartment with bars on the windows.

"Hey, we're here. Let's go," we said. My companion and I waited outside by the car, chatting about the nice weather Southern California always had. My companion was newly arrived in California, green, fairly sheltered, from a small town in Idaho. We waited for some time while the other missionaries finished packing their suitcases.

As we stood there, we noticed a small white Toyota driving slowly up the road. I thought, *Hmm, that seems odd; he seems to be going pretty slowly right through here.*

At that moment, as the car was in the street next to us, a man leaned out, brandishing a shiny handgun, and started to unload it, shooting at the house right across the street, ten to twenty yards from us.

Bang! Bang! Bang! his weapon loudly repeated.

His target was a man in his twenties in a driveway standing by a white van. Rather than hide, the man they were shooting at stepped out from behind his car, pulled a handgun from his waistband, and started shooting back—a real Wild West shootout.

A split second later, we dove behind our car and heard the back window of the car next to us explode into glass fragments as bullets slammed into it. The white Toyota getaway car squealed its tires as it rapidly accelerated down the street. We sat, shaken up, behind the car for several minutes to make sure it had quieted down.

I looked over at my companion and flippantly exclaimed, "Welcome to Southern California! Wasn't that exciting?"

He looked at me, slightly panic-stricken, pale, ashen white, and said, "Well, that's one way to say it." With a bit of a tremor in his voice, he then quietly asked me, "Does that happen all the time?"

I responded, "No. I was just kidding. First time for me to be that close to a shootout too. Let's hope it doesn't happen again!"

We quickly went inside and told the other missionaries, "Hurry up before we get shot at again!"

JALAPEÑOS FOR FUN

About halfway through my mission, I was assigned a companion named Lehi Alarco. He was Peruvian by birth and was raised in Australia. He was a great guy, very kind and creative, who loved comic books and cherry Slurpees. He also played acoustic guitar and taught me a few chords to strum on the guitar. His favorite song was "Iron Man." He taught me quite a bit about speaking Spanish as he had been raised bilingual, speaking Spanish and English. He also had an awesome Australian accent. When he would start speaking Spanish or English with his Australian accent with people on the street or when we were knocking on doors, he would get some perplexed looks.

As missionaries, we were very limited in our own recreational or fun activities. So one day when we were eating at a family's house, we noticed a large jar of pickled jalapeños on the table. Lehi and I glanced at the jar and looked at each other. "Let's have a jalapeño eating contest for fun," I suggested.

We unscrewed the top of the jar, and the strong smell of pickled jalapeños filled the air. They were complete jalapeños, stems, seeds, and all.

We each grabbed a jalapeño at the same time and popped it into our mouths, seeds and all. The pepper tasted as if it had been infused with burning kerosene. I felt the spicy burn spread through my mouth and nose as I slowly chewed it. My eyes started to water, my nose started to run, and my face flushed red with the searing pain from the burning pepper. I looked over at Lehi, and he didn't seem fazed at all. Not wanting to chicken out since it was my idea in the first place, I grabbed another pepper. To not be outdone, Lehi also grabbed another. As I chewed the second one, it felt as if a small inferno had been lit in my mouth and head.

A dozen jalapeños later, my mouth felt completely numb, my nose was running like a faucet, and my eyes were puffy, swollen, and full of tears. At this point, Lehi also seemed affected by the number of peppers he had eaten. We were both in a sorry state, looking and feeling like we had drunk lava from a volcano.

Feeling that I couldn't eat another fiery pepper, I suggested, "Let's call it a draw. I don't think I can eat anymore."

Lehi slowly nodded his head in agreement, and we called it a draw. A few minutes later, we left the house and thanked the family for their hospitality, hoping that the inferno in our heads would soon cool.

However, one thing we didn't count on was that the jalapeños just didn't go into our mouths; they were still in our bowels. When we were riding our bikes to our next appointment (maybe thirty minutes had passed), I really started to regret my entertainment choice as I felt the twisting inside; jalapeños were working their way through my system. My bowels voiced their complaints about my poor choice, churning into a fiery, crampy knot in my abdomen. A few minutes later, my colon screamed its wrath of displeasure, and I felt the strong urge to quickly find a bathroom.

Gratefully, at this time, we had arrived at our next appointment. I looked over at Lehi, and he seemed to also feel the ravages of the jalapeños twisting and turning in his gut.

As soon as the man opened the door, I quickly asked him, "Can I use your restroom? We had some bad food."

The gentleman looked at Lehi and me and quickly ascertained that we were in dire straits. He said, "Sure, come on in," and promptly escorted us to the bathrooms in his house.

I barely had time to sit before the liquid lava quickly exploded from my body like a fire hose with burning, melting heat. Fifteen minutes later, I felt as if I had undergone a complete colon cleanse, as anything and everything I had eaten the past few days had been explosively expelled. The bathroom smelled putrid, like an old outhouse that had sat in the sun for weeks.

Feeling embarrassed, I looked around for some air freshener. Thankfully, I found some and sprayed it around, trying to take the edge off the smell of swamp gas that filled the bathroom. I later heard of a joke that some Latinos use to describe the aftermath of eating jalapeños: sitting on the toilet yelling for the *bomberos* (firefighters) to come hose down the lava!

After our appointment, Lehi and I decided it would be better to walk home with our bikes than to sit on the bike seats.

SoCal Hospitality

The Latino people of SoCal were very kind to us. Many times, as we would knock on doors in the neighborhood, they would invite us in to have lunch with them, even if they didn't want to hear our message. Many of the church members would also invite us over for dinner. When we ate with them, they would spend more money than they could afford and would give us the nicest meal of the month, the best they could provide. It really humbled me to see their kindness. This again showed me the opposite of how I was raised, that there were good people in the world who were kind and would do nice things for others without any expectation of reward.

A couple of weeks later, as we canvassed a neighborhood, a Tongan family opened the door wide, and the mother said, "Come on in."

They were a large family with several adult sons living or staying with them. The sons, similar to us in age, looked like they played in the NFL. They were tall and muscular with warm, strong, welcoming handshakes. They shook our hands, welcoming us as strangers, inviting us into their family. Smells of delicious food greeted us as we stepped into the living room.

The mother continued, "We are just about to eat dinner. Would you like to join us?"

I responded, "Yes, absolutely. We are famished."

They invited us to sit down at their long family table, which sat upwards of twelve people. It looked as if they were having a feast. There were plates of food with pit-roasted succulent pork, *ota ika* (raw fish with coconut milk, onions, tomatoes, lemon juice), other fish, chicken, other meats (some wrapped in taro leaves with coconut milk), potato and chicken salad, coleslaw, *ufi* (yams), *kumala* (sweet potatoes), and, to top it off, fresh tropical fruit.

After we sat down, the mother of the family brought each of us a heaping dish of these wonderful delicacies piled into a small mountain on the plate. It was a much larger portion than we were accustomed to eating. However, it was incredible. The meat was cooked to perfection, each savory bite a delight on the palate, and the vegetables were roasted and crispy. I had never tasted food prepared so well. I felt transported, as if I were eating in a three-star Michelin restaurant. I relished each bite as I ate, grateful for the kindness of this family. I soon found myself quite satisfied as I finished the last of the food on my plate.

Seeing that I was finished, the mother stood up and filled my plate again with a heaping amount of the delectable dishes, kindly stating, "Here, Elder; have some more."

At this point, I was completely full of the savory food, not thinking I could eat any more.

One of the brothers laughed and said, "It's pretty good food, isn't it? My mom is a great cook."

I concurred. "Absolutely. I have never eaten such good food."

The mother beamed with pleasure. I wasn't sure that I could eat the second plate of food, so I looked at my companion, whose plate had also been refilled.

I shrugged, as if to say, *Well, we may as well get to work on eating it.* As it was so delicious, we actually ate the entire plate of food again.

As I finished the second plate, the mother looked over at me and kindly said, "Would you like some more?"

At that point, I felt I had eaten two Thanksgiving dinners, and I couldn't eat another bite. I graciously replied, "Thank you so much, but I can't eat another bite. I am so stuffed. Thanks so much for having us."

The woman and her kids smiled warmly at me, welcoming me as if I had been a part of their family for years.

These experiences of mingling with these wonderful people began to change me. They made me realize that what I had been taught as a child was incorrect—which was to fear everyone and that everyone was out to get you or use you in some way.

I continued to have my eyes opened and understood that many, many good people are in this world. I learned that I didn't need to be afraid, that life could be good, that I could trust people and believe in them. I feel this experience and these wonderful people changed my perspective and changed my life. Without this experience, I would have continued down my spiral of negativity and would have ended up in a bad place.

A Little McDonald's Can Go a Long Way

One afternoon a few weeks later, Lehi and I were walking along and noticed there was a person lying in a small alley between some old, beat-up buildings. The alley was dirt and gravel, strewn with trash, and filled with overgrown, unkempt weeds.

We grew concerned that something had happened to this person, and I told my companion, "We should go check on them to make sure they don't need help."

We headed towards the person lying at the end of the alley near a dumpster. When we arrived, we found it was a woman in her late twenties or early thirties, asleep or passed out. We gently tapped her shoulder to see if she was okay or needed help. She began to stir and woke up. She was disheveled, wearing clothes much too large for her small frame. She had unkempt blonde hair and a slight bruise around her right eye, and she was very thin—emaciated, a veritable living corpse.

I asked her, "Are you okay? Do you need us to call an ambulance?"

She slowly shook her head and replied, "No, I'm fine, but I'm very hungry. I haven't eaten in several days."

We did not have any food with us, so I told my companion, "Let's go find something for her to eat."

We walked down the street and found a McDonald's. I went in and used the money I was going to use for my lunch to get her some food. I ordered a burger, fries, and a Coke. It was the most I could afford on my meager budget, but I felt she needed to eat more than I did. We carried it back to her and sat on the ground in the garbage-filled alley in our shirts and ties, talking with her while she ate. We wanted to make sure she was okay and didn't need an ambulance.

She said, "Thank you. I wasn't sure how much longer I would last here, alone and lost."

I told her that God was real, that He lived, and that He loved us all despite what we had done or were doing, that she was a child of God and had value.

She shared with us, "I am sorry. I use drugs, and I need to get better but don't know how."

I glanced across the street and saw a shelter nearby. I told her, pointing across the street, "Let's go over there and see if we can get some help."

After she finished eating, we helped her to her feet and walked with her out of the alley to the shelter door. We knocked on the door and told them the situation, and they welcomed her into the shelter.

We never knew what happened to this woman, but I feel we were guided to her to save her life that day, to give her hope to change. Seeing her brought back vivid memories of my own time being homeless, spending the long, cold nights alone in the truck. The realization crept over me that without my sister letting me live with her, I would have been in the same state: broken, lost, living in some back alley.

Death Is Humbling and a Powerful Reminder

A couple of months later, we visited a family in our congregation. As we approached the house, we saw a very large pool of blood in the street. *What happened here?* we both wondered. The house was a small three-bedroom house with a chain-link fence and a small, well-kept yard with vivid multi-colored flowers and green grass. The house was painted with bright colors: yellow, red, and orange, mixed with some festive greens. The windows were covered with metal bars, and the front door had a metal steel screen protective door. We went up to the house slowly, walking past the blood pooling in the street, and knocked on the front door. A woman opened the door, and she was crying.

"*Pásense Hermanos,*" she said, sobbing. She continued, "*Mi amiga estaba de visita con nosotros y su pequeña hija, de solo dos años, salió corriendo a la calle y fue atropellada por un carro.*" ["My friend was visiting with us, and her young daughter, only two years old, ran out into the street and was hit by a car."] She then told us, "*Esta familia ha llegado recientemente a los Estados Unidos, desde México, solo habla Español y no Inglés.*" ["This family has recently moved to the US from Mexico, and they speak only Spanish and not any English."] She also related to us, "*No tienen papeles y tienen miedo. No saben qué hacer.*" ["They don't have papers (i.e., immigration papers, a green card). They are afraid. They don't know what to do."]

In short, this family had recently immigrated to the US from Mexico and were undocumented. They were afraid to go to the authorities for assistance. Many of the undocumented immigrants with whom we worked were afraid to go to the government authorities or police for anything they needed because they were afraid of getting deported. But it was our duty as missionaries to serve anyone in need, no matter where they were from or their legal status.

The woman was also a bit concerned about going to the authorities herself and asked us, "*¿Podrías ir al hospital y reunirte con ellos para traducirles para que sepan lo que está sucediendo?*" ["Could you go to the hospital and meet them to translate for them so they know what is happening?"]

The woman drove us to the hospital, and we met her friend and her friend's husband. We waited with them in the quiet hospital waiting room somberly without speaking, desperately waiting for any news of their daughter.

Soon the physician came into the waiting room and said in English, "I am sorry. We have done everything we could, but your daughter has passed away."

This young couple then looked at us to translate for them.

"*Lo siento, tu hija ha murio,*" I told them. ["I'm sorry, your young daughter has passed away."]

Little did I know then that this wouldn't be the last time I would have to tell parents that their child had died.

I don't remember much of anything else that was said after that. They were devastated and began sobbing. We tried to comfort them, but it was of no use as their only child had died.

I felt the waves of grief overwhelm me as well, as vivid flashbacks of my baby brother's death hit me like a tsunami. I remembered seeing him pulled out from the water, how cold his dead skin felt, and the long, terrible slow ride to the cemetery with his small body in the small child-sized coffin. I also broke down crying with them, and we hugged each other.

It was a tender moment, and I began to see with a more mature understanding how the death of Sammy had changed my mother. Before Sammy died, my mother had struggled with mental health issues. After he died, she completely shut down. She stopped going out into public and neglected the rest of us. Now, seeing what it was like firsthand as a child died and telling the parents this tragic news helped me to learn to feel some compassion for my mother. The anger and animosity I had carried for all these years began to dissipate, and the icy wall I had built around my heart began to melt as I began to forgive. It would take me years to do so fully, but I feel this was a big turning point for me.

I began to let go of the anger and leave it behind. I knew that despite everything that had happened in my life up to that point, I needed to let it go for myself because that anger was only poisoning me. If I kept drinking from the poisonous nectar of anger, it would lead to a double tragedy, and I would forever be dominated by that tragedy. For myself, I needed to let the past go. To have a future, I needed to give up the past and let go of the emotional baggage, to stop carrying the weight of the pain on my soul. I needed to move above and beyond the first tragedy and not make it the tragedy of my life that would ruin me, using the first tragedy as an excuse for everything that went wrong, wallowing in self-pity and tragically wasting my life.

MISSIONARIES DEAL WITH MALTREATMENT

During my mission, we had people treat us poorly too. I remember walking down a street one day, minding our business, when a car drove by. A young man in his twenties leaned out the window, yelled some obscenities at us, and threw his full thirty-two-ounce fruit punch soda at us, which hit us and splattered all over our clothes. Other times, we would have people spit at us as they drove by. Many, many people also slammed the door in our faces as soon as they saw who we were, often accompanying their disdain for us with an obscenity or two.

At the beginning of my mission, these experiences would make me angry or upset. Sometimes I would ask myself, *What am I doing here? I am spending my hard-earned money doing this?* (Missionaries are self-funded, spending their own or their family's money to support them on a mission.)

Toward the end of my mission, I had matured enough that I just felt bad for these people, people who felt so bad about themselves that they would lash out at two nineteen-to-twenty-year-old kids they had never met, strangers who were merely walking along the street. To me, these rude actions revealed their internal character and how bitterly they felt about themselves.

SoCal Earthquake

One particular night, I was suddenly awoken. The world was in motion. I sat up startled and saw the entire room was shaking, including my bed. The light was also swinging. In the next room, I heard crashes as dishes and glasses fell out of cupboards and shattered all over the floor. The realization hit me like a cold slap in the face.

"Earthquake!" I yelled to my companion, who was sleeping across the room from me.

The shaking persisted for several minutes. I sat there in awe of the powerful majesty of the earth as it rumbled, and I felt like an ant compared to it. I tried to stand, which was difficult due to the tremors in the earth.

Soon the shaking abated, and the world stopped moving. We looked around, went into the kitchen, and saw the shattered glass all over the floor and chairs tipped over. We were grateful that it had not been more severe. We later found out this was being called the Northridge earthquake, centered outside of Los Angeles, and it had been a 6.7 on the Richter scale. This quake caused a large amount of destruction and economic damage. It was the first time in my life I had experienced the raw power of nature and how powerless we are as humans to do anything when it is happening. It is something I will never forget, that hopeless feeling of seeing and feeling the awesome power of nature. After the quake, we called the members of our congregation to check on them and confirm that they were safe. Gratefully, they were.

The Last Christmas

On the last Christmas of my mission, we had been teaching a family who had recently emigrated from Guatemala. We found out they didn't have much money and were not going to be able to afford much for Christmas.

I told my companion, "We should help them out for Christmas and get them some things."

He agreed.

We decided to use our limited funds to get some presents. We went to the local grocery store and bought them a couple of weeks' worth of groceries. We then went to the toy store and bought some presents for their kids, including a doll and action figures. We then went to the department store and got the parents some clothes and a couple of other gifts. We didn't have a lot of money, but we spent everything we had to help them out.

We packaged up everything in a few boxes and walked to the family's house. We quietly put the boxes on their doorstep, rang the doorbell, and ran away to watch from a distance. They curiously opened the door and then opened the boxes. We saw tears of gratitude on the parents' faces and excitement and joy in the kids' faces.

The next day, we visited to check on them, and one of the kids told us excitedly, "Santa Claus came to our house last night and gave us presents! I got a doll and a teddy bear!" They also told us Santa Claus had brought them a lot of food.

The parents looked at us and asked, *"Elderes, ¿Sabes quién hizo esto por nosotros?"* ["Do you know who did this for us?"]

We did not tell them and simply said, "It's wonderful, but we have no idea who did that."

I think they suspected it was us, and with tears in their eyes, they said, *"Estábamos muy agradecidos con quien lo había hecho y les había dado una maravillosa Navidad. También dijeron que si averiguamos quién lo había hecho les agradecemos."* They were very grateful to whomever had done it, and it had given them a wonderful Christmas. They also said that if we found out who had done it to thank them.

RECIPROCAL NATURE OF A MISSION

My mission saved me. I went on my mission thinking that I would help people. In reality, what I learned was that when you lose yourself in service, you find yourself. You see and understand yourself and others more clearly. I did have the opportunity to help a lot of people, but those people showed me goodness, kindness, humility, and love. I learned to have faith in the human family and to trust in God. Others will fail us because they are human, but on God, one can always rely. I learned that I did not have to fear everyone, that there are good, kind people in the world, people of every race and religion who are just trying to live their lives and be good people. I learned that I could start to forgive and let the past be in the past, to not let the tragedy of my youth define me or hold me hostage forever.

With my mission drawing to an end after two years, I would have to figure out what I would do next. I had no money as I had used all I had made to serve my mission. I had lost my scholarship to the University of Utah. Therefore, in order to go back to school, I would have to rely on grants and student loans.

CHAPTER 17

Life after a Mission

IDAHO, HERE WE COME

My parents were now residing in Rexburg, Idaho. My older brother was working on his master's at Idaho State University (ISU) and living near them. He assured me that if I came to Idaho, he could help me get connected at ISU, so I decided Rexburg, Idaho, was to be my next destination. I applied to ISU and was accepted. ISU was actually an hour and a half away, so I decided to go to ISU Extension in Idaho Falls, which was only thirty minutes away. I arrived in Idaho from my mission at 11:00 p.m., and the next morning I started college.

For my ISU Extension classes, I would ride to school every day with my younger brother Aaron (we had decided to live with our parents to save money) in an old gray mid-1980s Chevrolet Monte Carlo that had well over a hundred thousand miles, probably close to two hundred thousand. I am sure we looked like a couple of rednecks who had grown up in the seventies, rolling down the road in the old Monte Carlo, listening to classic rock from the seventies and eighties. We had to drive with the windows down as the car did not have air-conditioning. The only thing we were missing were mullets. I didn't have a car, so I relied on my little brother and his car. For lunch, we would stop at a gas station and eat the cheap old hot dogs that were two for a dollar. They were not very good, but they sustained us, although healthy they were not.

Aaron and I took medical terminology together. In that class, we had to memorize definitions of medical words. He and I had a competition to get the highest grade in the class. Memorization is one of my strengths, so at the end of the semester, we had the two highest grades in the class. I often remind Aaron that I got the highest grade; I beat him by one or two points. We threw off the curve for the class as we both had a nearly perfect score for the semester.

Aaron and I became good friends, and it was nice to go to school with him and have that time together. I am three years older than him, so being classmates and good friends was a new experience for us. Aaron even helped me get a job working at the same McDonald's with him. I will always treasure those times I had with my brother.

Upon re-entering my university studies, I still was not sure what to major in. I had thought long and hard about my future during those cold nights back in the truck. Furthermore, on my mission, I extensively pondered what career I would enjoy undertaking. I figured it came down to two choices: either doing something on my own in science or helping people with science. I loved helping people, and I loved science.

I loved reading about Einstein, how he filled his lonely moments at the patent office writing out equations, trying to pierce the veil that separated the unknown from the known, or about Gregor Mendel at his monastery with his peas, basically discovering the entire field of genetics a whole generation before anyone else. But their work seemed very lonely, very isolated. I thrived in science, and I understood Isaac Newton's third law of motion, which states that for every action, there is an equal and opposite reaction. I learned that if I wanted to create a positive "reaction" in the world, I would first need to do something positive, to make a positive action forward.

My mission taught me that I actually liked being around most people, I needed people, and I needed to feel as if I were making a tangible improvement in their lives, to make a positive contribution to the world. Therefore, I concluded my career path had to help people in a positive way and to combine that with science.

SEEING "THE GIRL" AMIDST ETHICS DISCUSSIONS

When I returned from my mission, I enrolled in a college course called An Introduction to Allied Health Professions. The class was small with about twenty students, yet it covered a spectrum of careers in health care. I was hopeful that this class would help me know what I wanted to do with my life. Little did I know it would give me what I wanted and needed most. I would find the missing part of my soul, "my Teena."

The first day of class, a pretty red-haired girl with freckles named Gwen sat right next to me and immediately commenced to flirt. "Love your shirt!" she said. "Did you know that color really sets off your eyes?"

However, by then I'd already noticed the quiet girl who sat on the other side of the room, right in the first row. She was short and slim with blonde, flaxen hair (I'd heard that term *flaxen* before but never knew what it meant till the moment I set eyes on her). I also noticed that a stocky, muscular boy was always talking to her as if they'd known each other all their lives.

I sighed, *Oh well, she's taken.* I'd never pursue a girl if I had any inkling she might already be in a relationship, plus, because my home life was always such a mess, it really put a damper on my confidence. What was I going to say? How long could I deflect questions about my parents, my home life? It felt so shameful that I didn't even bother asking girls out, though, like most red-blooded American males, I thought about little else. I was already shy enough without worrying about taking a girl home to meet my angry, manipulative mom and my disheveled dad, as well as the clutter, the noise, the mess.

Part of the course was discussing and debating thorny medical ethical situations. We started with the "trolley dilemma." As described by Merriam-Webster, "The trolley problem is a thought experiment in ethics about a fictional scenario in which an onlooker has the choice to save 5 people in danger of being hit by a trolley, by diverting the trolley to kill just 1 person."

I remember thinking, *What are the chances that would happen to me?* Zero.

I didn't know how to divert a trolley in the first place, and if anyone were dumb enough to put me in charge of running a trolley, well, blood would be on their hands as well.

But the instructor posed it a different way. Had we ever had to choose the lesser of two evils? Why was it evil in the first place? These were things that appeared self-evident, but why was that so? Had we ever taken apart what we thought and brought it out into the light of day and looked at it? Really looked at it?

What if you were rolling down I-15 at seventy miles per hour at night and a row of red lights alerted you to an accident scene ahead? You hit the brakes—nothing. You press the brakes all the way to the floorboards—nothing. You have five seconds to decide who you are going to plow into. Is it going to be the car in front full of kids: four in the back seat, an infant in a car seat in the front, the driver a young mom? Do you swerve to the left: an older man hunched over the wheel? To the right: a middle-aged man and a young boy? Easy, huh? Of course you hit the old man. It's a question simply of age and numbers. Not so fast. What if the old man was a doctor on his way to the scene of an airplane crash? If he died, so did dozens of people. Changes things a little bit, huh? What if one of the vehicles in front was a big, sturdy truck?

Let's start counting the moral choices you must make, how much information you really have.

"It's a thought experiment," the instructor said. "So... think!"

Our individual groups chattered away the whole class time as if we could have talked all through the rest of the day and into the night. I began to realize ethics wasn't as simple a topic as it first appeared. Few things in this world are as cut and dried as we'd like. You've got to pick a few reliable principles and realize that they aren't always the right choices, but you must make the best choices you have at the moment with the information you have available.

I was always really looking forward to this class . . . and not just because of the lively discussions.

During the second-class period, we talked about euthanasia. We were assigned groups, and I got lucky; the blonde girl was assigned to mine. She sat opposite me and gave me a smile as she slid into her chair. That smile lit up the room. I was stunned for a moment. She was heart-stoppingly gorgeous. I hoped I didn't look like a slack-jawed yokel.

I found it hard to think, but I did think to use my peripheral vision, just as my coach had taught me in my younger years; that way I could satisfy my curiosity without giving myself away. (I had skills keeping a low profile.)

When I saw her, I thought to myself, *Wow. She has the most beautiful eyes. They are hazel, sometimes looking blue and sometimes looking green, with flecks of brown in them like gold dust. Her face is expressive, every feature so petite and delicate, her nose slightly upturned, her teeth gleaming. She has a smattering of freckles across her face like constellations.*

She said her name, and I said mine. Teena. Chris. *Teena, T-na. Tell me, have you seen her?* There was music in her name. Teena: I rolled those two syllables around in my mind. Was there a sweeter sound in this world? Not that I had ever heard.

Euthanasia. Tough topic. It was made tougher because the other woman in our group of four was a middle-aged, argumentative, coarse woman. The instructor gave each group several scenarios, but they all basically came down to this: The patient has no chance of recovering. They are in great pain. You push a button, a fatal dose of an opiate depresses their autonomic nervous system until they stop breathing and die peacefully, one last sigh as they leave this world.

The coarse woman said, "There's enough suffering in the world. If it was in your power to end their suffering humanely, why would you want them to continue to suffer? It seems cruel." Her voice was strident; the topic seemed very personal to her.

I tried to push back, gently at first. "Have you heard of the Hippocratic oath? First, do no harm. It's not a medical provider's job—in fact, it's the exact opposite of a doctor's job—to kill someone. It's pretty obvious that killing someone is harming them."

She jumped in, even more heatedly. "What if all their quality of life is gone and they want to end their life peacefully, surrounded by friends and family? You'd take that choice away from them? Condemn them to misery and suffering? What kind of an asshole would do that?"

I could feel myself getting heated, the flush of blood coming to my face as I began to match her angry energy with my own. "It's not your job. It's not your job to decide if someone lives or dies. It's the height of arrogance to think you can decide a matter of life or death."

"You don't know what you're talking about," she said. "Everyone is going to die. Not everyone gets to choose the time and place of their death. It doesn't have to be a miserable experience, going out howling in pain! If it was in your damn power to do something about it, you'd better damn well do something about it!"

I knew she was wrong, that my argument was right, clearer and more decisive. I for sure felt I would do everything in my power to save someone's life. But I felt myself growing silent. This woman was too angry, and I was having a bad enough day already to let her turn it into a disaster with my yelling at her for her obstinacy and vulgarity.

Then I heard Teena's voice—soft, almost a whisper. But her words were confident, assured. She shook her head. "I agree with Chris. It's not up to us to play God. That job is already taken. And what if people think they're being a burden and the pressure is on them to allow themselves to be euthanized? What if they're just having a bad day? What if they still have things to contribute? What if, even by their example, through their courage, they're providing us with value?"

Teena was speaking slowly, kindly, and compassionately. The other woman sputtered a bit, but it was clear she had no good comeback. She started to work herself up into an angry tirade but then sat back down. All of a sudden, she wasn't so strident when she realized that not everyone felt the same way as she did.

Thankfully, the instructor, hearing the woman's voice getting louder and louder, came to our rescue and changed the subject to something a little less controversial. I can't remember what it was exactly, but I remember clear as a bell how wonderful I felt that Teena had spoken up for me, a total stranger. Tee . . . na, T-nah, Teena. The chorus of the song: *Teena. Tell me, have you seen her?*

Oh yes, indeed I had.

I felt an instant connection. Not only was she beautiful, but she also agreed with me on this very fundamental issue. I'm not sure how I would have felt had she agreed with the vulgar woman. Probably not great.

We shared a smile as we sat back down, the instructor leading us into another thought experiment about ethics. I don't recall the specifics, but it was something about whether the greater good is served by harvesting a healthy person's organs to save a bunch of people's lives. That class was hard and provocative, but it introduced me to who would become the most important person in my life.

I looked forward to that class, the one bright spot in the struggle that was my life. I began to get my footing and confidence in my arguments. Bolstered by Teena's smile, I became assured and complete. When I stood up to talk, the class fell silent. They were actually interested in what I had to say. It couldn't have been more different than my family life.

About midway through the semester, I started to leave class one day. A small-framed man in his forties with an intimidating crew cut followed behind me. He got my attention and introduced himself. He said he wanted to introduce me to his daughter, Teena. Teena was just about to walk out the door when she heard her name and spun around. She immediately blushed and had what almost seemed like a look of horror. Her look turned into an awkward smile as she glanced over at me. She walked up to us and then, midsentence, the man just turned on his heel and abruptly walked away, leaving us fidgeting awkwardly.

I was about to blurt out something stupid, but Teena beat me to it with something that had been on my mind since the first time I'd laid eyes on her. "Would you like to go out sometime?"

"Yes. Yes, I would."

And so it began.

CHAPTER 18

Dating Life

WHAT'S A FIRST DATE WITHOUT A ROTTEN CHEESE SMELL?

Part of our allied health class involved getting CPR certified. Teena and I sat and talked about what we could do together and when we could do it. We quickly decided to go do the one-time CPR course together and get dinner afterward. Teena and I agreed that it would solve several problems at once: getting a school assignment done, learning a lifesaving skill, and, for a couple of earnest young kids without much money, making for an excellent first date, one we could relate over and over to our kids, grandkids, and, God willing, our great-grandkids. I was already thinking that way about Teena. I had no way of knowing how she felt about me, but so far, so good.

For the date, I prepared myself diligently. I took a quick shower with hot water (a precious resource in our family) and found some clean clothes, the best I could find: a pair of Levi's and a brown, black, and gray knit shirt. I borrowed the shirt from my younger brother as it was "community property," as we had no money to buy clothes for just one person. I then had to figure out a way to pick Teena up because I didn't have a car. I was too embarrassed to share how poor I was; I had only a couple of shirts and pants to my name.

Dad was very helpful. He offered me the use of the car, the beat-up Monte Carlo. Excited to have something to drive, I jumped in the car, already running behind yet planning excitedly for the date. I drove several miles singing along to eighties rock on the radio when one of my favorite songs played: "Don't Stop Believin'" by Journey. I sang along:

Just a small town girl

Livin' in a lonely world...

Just a city boy...

He took the midnight train going anywhere...

Don't stop believin'...

As I hit the chorus, a strange, unpleasant odor overtook my senses, a noxious odor, not quite as bad as the jalapeño incident from my mission but close. I discerned the smell of sweaty feet or moldy cheese. Worse, it was actually a combination of both! Knowing my family, I quickly figured out it was likely the smell of milk or ice cream spilled somewhere on the floor that had never been cleaned up, left to percolate, brewing in the sun, ripening to a smell that reminded me of the locker room in high school after practice. In short, this was my nightmare happening in real life. I didn't have any time to try to clean it as we had to make the CPR class on time, so I drove on, opening the windows, hoping (might I say praying?) that most of the smell would leave the car before I got to Teena's house.

By the time I arrived, I couldn't smell the odor anymore, likely numbed to it. I walked up to the door, hoping my clothes didn't smell like the blue cheese aisle at the grocery store, and slowly knocked on the door.

When Teena answered, I said, "Ready? Let's go."

She sweetly smiled and said, "Sure, let's go."

I opened the car door for her, and she jumped in with a smile.

She was a perfect date, asking me, "How was your day? How is class going?" She made small talk the whole way to the fire station where the CPR class was being held.

When we arrived, we found the room where our class was being conducted. It was a small, old training room in the fire station, with old, graying white tiles. They had spread some old carpets on the floor for the class. I looked around and saw five or six other students also there to get CPR certified. I noticed the handful of half-torso plastic training mannequins—"Resuci Anne"s—spread out across the floor and thought, *Umm, maybe this wasn't the best idea for a first date.*

The instructor, a no-nonsense nurse in her mid-forties, dressed in scrubs, with brown hair and a face that said, *I mean business; don't mess with me*, invited us to take our seats on the floor by the mannequins. It was my first introduction to learning the art of saving lives.

"Anne, Are You Okay?"

The instructor taught us CPR on Resusci Anne, the life-sized plastic doll that we would all take turns resuscitating. How awkward it felt to be in the middle of the class yelling, "Anne, Anne, are you okay?! Someone call 911!"

Then the compressions began. I remember that they were to be the same beat as the classic Bee Gees anthem "Stayin' Alive": "Ah, ha, ha, ha, stayin' alive, stayin' alive." One and two and three and four and . . . two breaths, watching her chest inflate. The process continued. I think my face must have been a shade of crimson as I thought about the whole class watching me, especially Teena.

As I practiced "saving" Anne, I became thoroughly convinced that I had taken Teena on the worst first date of all time, especially with the pungent moldy cheese smell to top it off.

Finally, the class came to an end. We passed, but more importantly, the embarrassment ended too.

First Date: Phase Two

Teena and I walked out of the fire station feeling the warm sun of a beautiful day on our faces, relieved to be headed toward a more typical date. Even after the "CPR and moldy cheese" fiasco, Teena was still smiling at me, still laughing at my feeble attempts at humor, her sandy blonde hair gleaming in the noontime sun, so somehow I guessed we had gotten through the CPR class without jeopardizing our new relationship. Phew. What kind of clodhopper would take a girl he really liked to CPR training? I mean, seriously. Apparently me!

Sometime later, I found out that Teena actually has a far above average ability to detect smells, almost like a superpower. She had quickly smelled the "moldy cheese," which I also later found out was coming from the floor on her side of the car. She was at ground zero of the noxious fumes. Teena confessed that she had assumed I had smelly feet but was horrified and worried that I might think it was her feet that were stinky. She'd thought, *Boy, if this guy has stinky feet, hopefully, we can become good enough friends that I can throw away his socks and soak his feet in black tea and Epsom salts.*

We drove to a restaurant called Papa Kelsey's, a local sandwich shop. It had typical sandwich shop decor, with posters advertising the special of the week, wooden tables and chairs spread around the room, a counter, and a menu on the far wall. The shop was simple but nice, nothing fancy or expensive. Neither of us could afford anything else. But of course, I didn't know that about Teena yet.

We walked up to the counter and ordered our subs. I was relieved that Teena didn't choose anything too expensive.

Without hesitation, Teena said, "I would like a ham and Swiss sandwich."

Being somewhat indecisive and not knowing what to order, I thought that sounded good. I responded with "We'll take two of those," and I paid for the lunch.

Teena then turned and walked straight to a quiet, secluded booth off to the side. To this day, we always look for the quiet, secluded booth. This would be the first time I got to hang out with Teena outside of a class-room, and it was much better than the CPR class. I felt a little nervous, not knowing what I would say and feeling awkward after having "saved" Anne the dummy.

But once we started talking, the conversation just flowed from topic to topic. I had never known anyone so easy to talk to, so kind, and such a generous listener. Teena made me feel as if I were the most important person in the world. I reflected that back to her, mirroring her gestures, her smiles, her laughter. It was the most natural thing in the world.

We chattered away happily long after our food was gone. After lunch, I walked out into the dazzling sun of the parking lot, feeling as if I'd known this woman my entire life.

She said, "Do you want to come back to my house and watch a movie?"

"Sure. That sounds great."

Teena's house was a neat ranch-style home in a quiet cul-de-sac with a beautiful rose garden in front: a rose-covered arch, roses climbing along a trellis, roses perfuming the air. Teena set up the VCR to play Disney's *The*

Lion King. I had never seen it, and I was quite excited to do so. Even more so, I was with this incredible woman with whom I had felt an immediate connection.

I had some clues that my feelings were being reciprocated. Teena felt comfortable enough to lean her head on my shoulder, and soon she was fast asleep, this beautiful angel; her perfect face resting on me in complete trust; her nose, her eyes, her long lashes, her hair framing her face as if in a painting no artist on this earth had the talent to capture. Her breathing was soft and easy. I could stare to my heart's content. I wanted to put my arm around her, this delicate creature, but I felt that it was too soon, too fast. I didn't dare scare her off—not this one, not after waiting a lifetime.

The Circle of Life indeed.

As I watched the movie, I felt like Simba when he found Nala. Simba wonders if Nala can ever love him because of his past. I felt the same way and wondered if anyone would ever love me because of my past.

The movie ended too soon. Simba defeats Scar, then reunites with Nala, and they have a cub. Simba's legacy continues, and all live happily ever after. Simba finds his true love and learns to accept his past. As I watched Teena, I wondered if this was my chance to find true love and acceptance of my past.

Teena woke up after the movie ended and walked me to the door. My heart raced a little at the thought of maybe getting a goodnight hug. *Slow down, buddy. You've got time. Get to know her. I've got a feeling she's the one,* I said to myself.

Teena said, "Thank you for the ride and the lunch. It was fun. Let's do it again soon."

I smiled. "Of course. But no CPR class next time!"

We shared a laugh.

She asked, "I like to go rock climbing and rappelling with my friends. Would you like to go? It's fun!"

I thought, *Hanging off a cliff with a skinny rope with my fear of heights? How is that fun? I don't think so! My fear of heights is perfectly rational! Heights kill!* But I heard myself saying enthusiastically, "Yes, let's do it!"

We never did go rappelling.

DATE NUMBER TWO

On our next date, we grabbed Subway sandwiches and went to the Idaho Falls Greenbelt—a scenic walkway between the Snake River and the falls. The river sparkled as the sun reflected off the water. The sound of the water going over the falls was calming as the light breeze gently blew. Teena had a serious look on her face and wasn't saying much. It was nothing like our first date. I wondered what must be on her mind.

Finally, she said, "You know, Chris, I have to be completely honest with you. I want to go on a mission, so I am not interested in getting into a serious relationship right now. Is it alright that we be good friends?"

I felt a piercing pain in my chest, stabbed in the heart. Wow, I wasn't expecting that, not the "not a good time for a serious relationship" speech. I felt my throat constricting, my heart pounding. But I acted as nonchalantly as I could.

"That's fine, Teena. I totally think it is great for you to go on a mission. I don't want to get serious either. Not a good time for me. I've got to focus on my studies. And that's hard for me with this pretty face distracting me."

She laughed, then sighed. "Chris, I'm glad that we can be friends."

I thought, *Still be friends? Wait, I invented the "let's still be friends" speech!*

Truth is, I felt relieved and good about that conversation. Having just gotten back from a mission, I was excited that Teena wanted to have that experience, and I loved and admired that she was the kind of person who would want to go serve. It made me like her even more. I also felt relieved that I wouldn't have to worry about what would happen next between us. We could just be ourselves and have fun, no need to worry about second-guessing anything. I knew that beyond any romantic consideration, of which I had experienced little, we would be good friends.

Easy.

A BUDDING "FRIENDSHIP"

My parents' financial troubles continued, and we couldn't afford a phone line. So I couldn't call Teena as much as I would have liked. I looked forward to the classes because there was Teena with her long lashes and her bright smile. It was the best part of my day. I wanted to talk to her all day every day. In the evenings, I would scrounge up seventy-five cents from my earnings. Then I would walk two-plus miles to the gas station to use the pay phone to call Teena. Of course, she didn't know that I didn't have a phone. It was embarrassing, and I was not about to tell her. If I told her, I wondered if she might think I was some strange person. I told myself, *Who doesn't have a phone in the world today? Most folks do. Even when I was a poor missionary, we had a phone.* More importantly, if I told her, I was afraid she would know that I liked her more than as a friend, which is not what she wanted at that time.

When I would call from the pay phone at the gas station, most of the time it was awkward. The conversations were usually just getting started when the operator's voice would cut in: "Please deposit more coins to continue."

Each time, I told myself, *Ugh, already? Where did the three minutes go?*

Most days, I didn't have more coins, so I would make up some lame excuse to get off the line before the call was cut off. I worried that Teena would think I was not interested in her or that I did not know how to make conversation. I really wanted to get to know her better, but three-minute conversations don't allow for deep, soul-searching conversations!

I had a best friend. Her voice was the sweetest thing I'd ever heard: the way she would talk about the teachers, the other students, studying, whatever it was. She never had an unkind word for anyone. We talked about class, about the internationally-known murderer, Gary Gilmore, who demanded his death sentence and was executed in 1978, and how he defiantly stood when the firing squad lined up.

"Let's do it," he said.

Teena said he'd had a hard raising, moving around a lot, poor family, his dad always in trouble. Wow, he sounded like me. How come I wasn't out there killing people?

I reminded Teena of the horrible murders he'd committed, a true psychopath. She said, "I'm sorry, Chris. I just don't have it in me to have hard feelings towards anyone."

I felt the truth of what she was saying. With all these questions of what justice is and how it is served, I was glad I wasn't a judge.

What I couldn't share with Teena was my poverty, that I didn't have a phone or a car, that I shared a room and most of my clothes with Aaron, that I slept in a barely converted garage with a concrete floor on a bed as hard as that floor, that I spoke only for two minutes at a time because the operator was going to cut off the phone call. I was afraid, afraid that by sharing with her who I really was, I would lose her, as I had lost so many friends and family members before.

I knew I was going to have to come clean at some point. It gnawed at me. Those moments Teena and I shared in class and on the phone were far and away the best things in my life. But I felt like an impostor, a fraud. I couldn't bear the thought of not having that dazzling smile in my life, her soft scent and sweet voice.

Teena asked me for my number many times, and I deflected. "Oh, sorry, I've got to go. My brother is waiting," or "Okay, I'll call you instead."

I was beginning to lose sleep over trying to maintain the facade as I had always done.

After class, Teena and I lingered as we often did. We would walk for miles from the school down to the Greenbelt. It was our favorite place and our favorite thing to do—walk and talk for hours. We became the best of friends. We talked about our dreams and desires, about everything—everything except what loomed over me.

My heart would leap out of my chest like a caged bird with each talk we had. I begged myself, *Just come out with it, Chris. You know she's got loads of empathy. It's what you love about her!*

Teena never had a problem sharing about herself with me. She told me how her parents had been injured, unable to work, and being put on disability. She told me how they didn't have money for Christmas presents or Thanksgiving dinner in years past, and how she had also worked hard just to pay for necessities. She told me without shame or hesitation, almost as if to say, *Hey, this is me, and I'm not ashamed of it either.*

So why was it so hard for me to just be vulnerable and let her see where I really came from? Well, the day finally arrived; I decided I would tell her.

I leaned forward, put my trust in her, and let it go.

"Teena," I said, "I can't give you my number because I don't have a phone. I couldn't figure out how to tell you because I'm embarrassed."

She smiled, grabbed my arm, and leaned into my shoulder. "I don't care that you don't have a phone, Chris," she said.

I nearly wept with relief. She just kept on talking as if it were nothing, as if she hadn't given it a second thought. She looked at me and smiled, and all of the tension I had was . . . gone. I had underestimated her—and not for the last time.

After finding out I did not have a phone, Teena began to show up regularly at my door, shrugging off the half-hour drive each way. It felt wonderful to know that someone like her cared so much for me that she would literally go out of her way to spend time with me as often as possible.

I had always assumed that because Teena lived in a nice home, her family was on sound financial footing, but due to her parents' poor health stemming from accidents, their finances were compromised. I began to realize that although she hadn't been homeless, hadn't gone hungry, hadn't moved countless times, Teena had to work for everything she needed and everything she wanted. Because of this, she understood my situation better than I had realized. There was no worry, no judgment, no confusion between us, just trust, compassion, and empathy. It made our friendship so easy and so wonderful.

The things we did together were inexpensive, yet we always lived well in our own way. Most of this was thanks to her. Teena had a sense of style and a flair for turning the mundane into the elegant that I sorely lacked. We could not afford fancy, but she had a way of bringing fancy to us.

One afternoon, she showed up at school with a picnic lunch. She asked me, "Would you like to have a picnic with me on this lovely day?"

"Of course I would."

We left the classroom and went out and sat by the banks of the Snake River on the green grass under the sunshine. I watched (with my stomach growling) as Teena unpacked a basket with fresh strawberries, marshmallow dip, and strawberry cream cheese, something I had never tried but became a fan of with the first bite.

As we often did, we discussed life, dreams, and hopes for the future. Teena, a compassionate soul, clearly wanted to make a difference and to impact the lives of others in a positive way.

We had become friends first. We didn't discuss it directly, but we knew our relationship was blossoming into much more. It felt as though we had always known each other, and my earlier life without her began to feel like a distant memory. I hadn't held her hand or kissed her, but I felt that she was my soul mate, and it happened so unexpectedly, effortlessly, and in a mere blink of an eye. I never believed in these types of things—soul mates, destiny, fate—but I was starting to. It was almost as if we had known each other a whole earlier lifetime, and I had just been wandering aimlessly until we were reunited once again.

CHAPTER 19

From Friendship to Relationship

One evening, we were at Teena's grandmother's home after a day of playing pool and eating good food. As we sat on the sofa watching *The Price Is Right*, the sounds of the television seemed to fade into the background, and our focus was totally on each other.

Teena said, "If someone has feelings for someone else, they should act upon those feelings."

I gathered she was saying something meaningful, but I wasn't exactly quick on the uptake or in any hurry to take action. What if I were rejected? What if it ruined our friendship? Was she saying I should hold her hand? Was she implying that when we said goodbye that day, I should act upon my desire and look into her eyes and kiss her?

Wracked with doubt, I said, "But what if the other person doesn't want that?"

Could she possibly have felt the same way I felt about her?

"One will never know unless one tries!" she blurted without even a moment's hesitation.

The room seemed suddenly very hot. My heart thumped in my chest as I thought about holding her, touching her hand, kissing her. It was as though there was a tangible warmth and energy swelling in my body and expanding to fill the entire room.

Then her grandma walked in.

Well, that did it. Poof! Like a puff of smoke, the moment was gone. It was time for me to leave.

One moment we were about to kiss, and the next . . . we were outside heading towards my car.

I told myself, *I have to hold onto her this time. Now is the moment.* I strived to raise up the courage. I didn't know exactly what I was going to do or say, but I still had that energy, that burning desire surging through me.

As had become our custom, Teena put her arms under mine, hugged me, and said goodbye. But this time, I didn't let her go. I didn't say goodbye.

I held her close, breathing in her sweet scent of vanilla. My heart was pounding in my chest from anxiety and anticipation. I looked down into her eyes as though I were looking into eternity, she into mine. Then slowly our lips came together as we both made that next move together. It was magical. Her lips were the sweetest thing I had tasted, her eyes deep pools of hazel that captured my breath.

Things had changed for us, changed forever. We hadn't planned on this. Some call it fate, some destiny. What started out as friendship became so much more. I knew I loved her before I had ever even held her hand. I never thought that a relationship could be so easy and feel so right.

But it wasn't all smooth sailing.

At this point, Teena's family had moved away to Montana. She was now living alone in her parents' home, which was about to be sold. I realized she was stressed about this. Where should she live?

One day, Teena came to me and explained, "I've decided I'm not going to serve a mission. My cousin has offered me to come live with her down in Salt Lake City. I can work for my cousin's husband there. They will let me live with them and pay me too. I can transfer and go to school there."

In summation, she would have housing and pay, which meant money, and she would be able to continue school in Salt Lake. Clearly, she was nervous as she said this. And so was I.

My heart sank. Would she leave me? Would this be the end? What was she saying? Salt Lake was four hours away, and seeing each other on a regular basis would be terribly impractical if not impossible. I didn't even have a phone or a car.

She said, "I love you, Chris. But I can't pass up this great opportunity."

The idea of losing her seemed unbearable. Yet how could I ask her to pass up a great opportunity?

Of course, I had been thinking for some time about asking Teena to marry me. But I had thought there was no hurry. I was not sure I was ready either. Now, with this news, I was in a panic just at the thought that she would be gone, would be so far away.

I held her hands and faced her. I said, "I have to go to Oregon for the weekend to attend my brother's wedding. Wait to decide what to do until I get back."

I felt a bit of a reprieve when she said, "Okay."

Teena Gave Me a Scare, but Joy Followed

That weekend, all I could think about was how I wanted to be with Teena—all the time. I began to pray, asking to know what I should do. It was so important that I make the right decision, that I say the right thing to her when I got home. It was one of the most important decisions of my existence. But perhaps it was not such a difficult decision after all. As I thought through everything, I knew I had already made the decision in the back of my mind long before that weekend. I should marry her!

Yet one of my greatest worries was that I simply didn't have much to offer Teena. Practically speaking, I had nothing. But I had to put myself out there and take the risk that she would not reject me. I had to be confident in myself knowing that, moving forward, I would be able to provide a comfortable and stable lifestyle for her. Without her, I would be only a fraction of a person, like a part of me was missing. I was certain we were meant to be together. I couldn't be certain that she felt the same way, but it seemed so.

I felt at peace with this decision and found strength in the assurance and anticipation that I would go home and ask her to marry me, to be with me forever, and she would say yes. And we would make it work. I needed to lean forward and leap, trusting in her.

The drive back from Oregon seemed to take forever, but it was almost as if there were a magnetic pull, summoning me back to where I belonged, back with Teena.

As soon as I got back to the house, I borrowed Aaron's car and immediately drove to Idaho Falls. As I drove, I went over different ways I might propose to Teena. I decided that I should do it where we had already spent so much of our time, along the Greenbelt of the Snake River, where we often walked, talking about the future, a perfect location with a view of the beautiful church temple where our future could become one future in marriage . . . that is, if she said yes. We had so many good memories of that area already, this seemed like the perfect plan.

Then my concerns became more immediate. I drove to Teena's home not even knowing if she would be there. I knocked on the door, and there she was, a beautiful angel. It was another lovely day, so I asked if she wanted to go for a walk. As it turned out, I was in for a bit of a shock.

Teena told me that she had quit her job and was preparing to leave for Salt Lake City.

Wait, what?

She hadn't waited for me to get back from Oregon? This wasn't a good sign. I felt panic return. But then, I decided, so much for the plan. This was an emergency!

When we reached the corner on the sidewalk, I said to Teena, "I have good news and bad news."

Her eyes widened.

I paused a moment for effect.

"Yes?"

"The good news is I've come to a decision. The bad news is you're going to be stuck with me for a very long time."

With that, I dropped to one knee, looked into her eyes, took her hand, and asked her to marry me.

She smiled and cried all at once, and she said, "Yes!"

We held onto each other for dear life. I didn't have a ring yet, but that could wait. Everything could wait now. We had each other.

We spent the rest of the afternoon and evening talking about the ring, the wedding, and how we were going to make it all happen. It was a great night. Both of us were so excited about our future together.

The next day, we went to the mall, found a jewelry store, and looked at different rings. Of course, we were very limited in funds, so Teena picked out a simple but beautiful rose gold ring with a rose on top, a diamond in the middle. I got a gold band.

My Mother's Never-Ending Disapproval

I waited for some time to tell my family the news. My two older brothers were both recently married (it was one of their weddings I had attended in Oregon). My older brother, David, was always one of Mom's favorites. Mom loved his new wife, who was studying speech pathology. Johnny's new wife had also earned Mom's seal of approval, especially since she was from a well-off family and was studying nursing.

But for me, who for some reason my mother seemed to think could never do well or do enough and who was a "difficult child," I had no idea how she would react. Not only did I expect her to project her own inadequacies onto me as she had so often done, but I expected her to use her well-practiced manipulative ways to control me as she had done in the past. I knew that she depended on me for financial support as I would give my parents my student loan money and help my family out financially as best as I could as a college kid working in fast food. A wife would only soak up my financial resources.

With these considerations, I held off telling my family about my wedding plans. I shared our plans in dribs and drabs. Eventually, I broke the news when Teena and I both signed the card to my older brother's wedding gift as a couple. That triggered some questions from Mom.

"Are you two serious?" Then, later, "Are you thinking of getting married?"

Finally, I told Mom that Teena and I were engaged.

Mom's response? "You cannot be serious with anyone! You must be joking."

She added that I was too young to get married, although she had been younger than I, only eighteen, when she was married. She laughed it off, acting like I was ridiculous. She implied I couldn't handle marriage.

At this point, I was twenty-one years old and more than halfway toward my degree after only a year of college, and I had spent two years as a missionary in crime-ridden areas of Southern California. I had already witnessed more things than many people would see in their lifetimes. I'd helped gang members leave the gang life behind. I'd been on my own since I was seventeen, and I had worked most of my life, since the age of eight. I was far more mature and seasoned than most men my age, if nothing else than out of necessity.

Mom began a relentless, unending emotional assault in an attempt to stop my wedding. She insisted I would screw up my life and never achieve anything. She tried to convince me that I could not afford to be married . . . interesting considering that my parents were not shining examples of financial stability and they relied on my income.

When my mom couldn't convince me, she went to work on Teena. One day when Teena was over and I had gone to the bathroom, Mom told Teena that marrying me would ruin my life, that she didn't have a degree and would hold me back.

I thought I would be immune to such blatant manipulation of the kind that I had seen time and again during my life, but in fact, I wasn't. She was my mother and had a powerful effect on me, no matter how much I attempted to resist.

After the continuous onslaught of mind games, I eventually fell under the shadow of her manipulation. I went to Teena and told her perhaps we should wait to get married so I could work, save money, and be financially ready for marriage.

She took off the ring, gave it back to me, and said, "Well, then, you can go marry your mother!"

That did it. It was like a bucket of cold water being poured over my head. I immediately woke from the emotionally brainwashed zombie state that my mother had created. I was not about to delay my happiness with Teena. And I would not give in to my mother and return to the shell of unhappiness that I had shouldered most of my life. Teena was the light of my life, made me whole, made me feel like a real person with a real chance at happiness.

I immediately told Teena she was right, I was sorry, and we were going to get married as planned. We then went and told Mom that we were not about to change our plans to get married. When I left the room for a moment, Mom began to attack Teena, piling on once again with claims that she would be ruining my life. She drew the line. I had to choose between her and Teena.

I chose Teena.

Although being at home with Mom while she was giving me the silent treatment was uncomfortable, it cemented my desire to situate myself as soon as possible so I could get out of that house and live with Teena.

Up to that point, most of my money from working and student loans had been passed along to my parents in an attempt to keep my family afloat. But here's the thing: Teena and I were both used to being poor, used to carrying so much burden on our shoulders, far beyond our years, that we didn't expect much. We knew how to do without. All we needed was each other. And we would get by on the practical matters one way or another.

For the first time in our lives, we were no longer alone in carrying our enormous burdens. Teena gave hers to me, I gave mine to hers, and it seemed for the first time ever in my life that the burden was light and I could breathe.

One evening, Teena left my house to head home, and her car wouldn't start. Right across my house was an auto repair shop. My dad said that was the best place to take it, so we pushed the car across the street. The owner of the shop seemed so helpful and happy to take Teena's car and work on it. He said he would have to order a part, and it would take a few days.

I was back to having to borrow Aaron's car so I could see Teena. She was no longer able to get anywhere because her family now lived in Montana. We were anxious to get her car back.

A few days later, we showed up at the repair shop as instructed by the owner, and he led us to Teena's car. As we looked at it, I felt my stomach drop, and anger began to swell inside of me. The mechanic had stripped her car of any valuable parts, and her car was literally in boxes. The man proceeded to tell us that my parents had ripped him off and that he would not return the parts until he was paid.

What would Teena think? She knew that we struggled financially, but I never told her even half of it. Now she knew what kind of people my parents were, and because of it, she was affected as well. We simply didn't have the money to pay the guy, and now we didn't have a car either.

Teena was upset, but not even for a minute did she blame me. She didn't look back even for a moment. We didn't know what to do. (Looking back, I wish that we had called the police.) We sat down and decided we would walk away from the situation and take out a loan to buy a car. Teena had established credit and had connections at her bank, so she got the loan, and we picked out a car together.

We proceeded with our wedding plans. The total cost of the wedding would be: $250!

We lined up a place to live in Idaho Falls where we didn't have to come up with a deposit (Teena's cousin was renting it out). Teena also had a car again and had quickly regained employment as a developmental therapist once she knew she would not be going to Salt Lake City, so we were covered on several fronts. We would have what we needed.

After a month, Mom finally accepted that I would get married. Despite all the troubles from her, I was glad she was coming around. She began to ask about our plans and dates. Then the mind games began anew.

"You can't get married that day."

"I want to do the reception for you, but this date won't work."

"Can you push back the date?"

We tried to accommodate her on the date, but the church wasn't available, perhaps not coincidentally on any dates that she chose. To this day, my wife sometimes struggles to remember on which day we were actually married because my mother had insisted upon changing the date so often. But even my mother could be worn down eventually. She finally agreed upon a date and informed us that she would have a "nice reception" planned for us.

CHAPTER 20

Wedding Day and
"Wedding Receptions"

THE BIG EVENT-FILLED DAY ... AND A FLAMING RED DRESS

Our wedding day was—finally—only a few days away. Teena and I were thrilled. Teena had visited the temple the night before our marriage in preparation for the big day. Because my parents were always late, I did not trust they would get me to the wedding on time. So wisely, I spent the night at Teena's grandparents', and she and I stayed up most of the night talking with great excitement and anticipation about the morning that awaited us, when we could finally step over the threshold, stop being a lonely "I," and forever become an "us."

When morning arrived, we readied ourselves and went to the temple. We encountered a surprise that really wasn't one, or shouldn't have been. We waited and waited... My parents never showed.

Naturally, embarrassment washed over me as Teena's extended family saw that my own parents hadn't bothered to show up for my wedding. In my heart, this was compounded by knowing that just several months earlier, my parents had gone to the temple, supporting my brothers when they had been married. They had even thrown nice receptions for them.

I looked up at my beautiful wife dressed in white beside me, and my feelings of sadness vanished. It didn't matter that my parents hadn't shown. That was just who they were, not who *I* was. I was on the threshold of a sea change in my life that would bring me the kind of happiness I had thought I would never find.

As it turned out, the moment of our marriage, and the entire day, could not have been more perfect. My sister Darlene's husband, Stan, stepped up to be my family and participate in the ceremony. As we were married, I gazed into Teena's hazel eyes, and I glimpsed a small part of her eternal love for me. As the ceremony concluded, I looked up and noticed that the mirror behind her was perfectly aligned with a mirror that was behind me, and as that mirror reflected the one behind me, I saw a virtual representation of Teena and I going on and on forever. My parents' failure to show up, the room, the people, all of it and everyone around, just seemed to fade into the distance. I felt a happiness, a completeness, an acceptance I had never experienced before. Joy, peace, and security would be mine. No, better than that, it would be *ours* at last.

After the ceremony, we made our way outside for photos to capture a memory that would forever be a reminder of that perfect wedding.

And then, *she* arrived.

My mother.

She strutted towards us like the star of the show, dressed in a flaming red dress and fishnet stockings, blonde hair ratted up like a fangirl from Bon Jovi's entourage. I didn't know which was more embarrassing: the fact that my parents hadn't shown up for my wedding or that Mom had finally shown up after it looking for all the world like an eighties rock groupie.

The party could start now; the *star* had arrived!

I did my best to ignore Mom, but come on! She had expertly altered one of the most beautifully sublime moments of my life, changing it into something negative with the spotlight focused on her in her ridiculous outfit. She was impossible for anyone to miss as the center of attention.

The first of the "receptions," plural, began.

Neither Teena nor I got what we wanted for receptions—not that that was terribly important to either of us. Teena had planned to have an outdoor reception in a beautiful little garden area at her church. But her father had insisted we do it inside just in case it rained, even though there was not a cloud in the sky and it had not rained in weeks.

We found ourselves in a sparsely decorated church gymnasium, a basketball court with lines on the floor and white cinder block walls. It didn't look as nice as the garden, but still, we made the best of it. Teena and I enjoyed what became a family reunion with her extended family as we spent a few hours greeting everyone. We finally cut the simple cake that Teena's aunt had made. Everything was simple and plain in the gym, but we didn't care. Teena and I just looked at each other, eagerly waiting for all of it to be over so we could finally be alone together, husband and wife.

But first, there would be one more "reception" to attend.

My mother's.

THE SECOND "RECEPTION"

The second reception was to be the "nice one" that Mom had planned, just like the one she had organized for my brothers, with all the decorations and the "real" wedding cake.

We had to travel thirty minutes to reach the church where Mom had "set things up." When we arrived, we noticed the parking lot was full of cars. We wondered, *Was our reception already packed with people?* Then, as we got out of the car, we noticed people out on the lawn having a big party, wearing jeans and flannel shirts, cowboy boots, and giant rodeo belt buckles, looking like a bunch of Idaho farm folk, which is what most of them were.

It was a church party . . . a church summer barbeque get-together . . . completely unrelated to our wedding!

In the middle of all the farmers sat my parents, eating barbecue. Mom acted as though this had been the plan. She didn't bat an eyelash or display any sorrow, embarrassment, guilt—nothing.

She shouted, "Hey! Go get some food!"

It might not seem possible, but things got weirder. . . "going off the rails on a crazy train." The song from my youth flashed in my mind. At that moment, someone announced they were going to have a wheelbarrow race, to be run by four of the most recently married couples at the party.

Mom shouted, "These two were just married this morning!" and wildly gestured at us.

Teena and I exchanged, *What the he**??* looks, as though we had wandered into some dystopian alternate reality.

I didn't know if Mom's plan had been to humiliate us on our wedding day, get the last laugh, or just show me that even though I was now married and on my own, she would always be there, ominously in the shadows, a wraith, a specter, always haunting me.

I was ready to leave at that point, but the fact was we had been publicly put on the spot and now manipulated into participating in a wheelbarrow race. Some of the farmers ushered us over to where the other couples were getting ready for the race. Teena was coaxed into a wheelbarrow as I was blindfolded. The wives were instructed to lead their husbands through an obstacle course, the blindfolded husbands relying on instructions from their wheelbarrow-mounted wives to make it through the course alive, reach the finish line, and win the race.

Neither Teena nor I had ever seen this sort of thing before. With the exchange of a single glance, we simply decided to have fun with it. And we actually won the race! Teena was a sport. I would not have blamed her for becoming a runaway bride before that day was over, but she didn't, and she was ready to make the best of that strange moment. Mom, trying though she might have been to sabotage our day, had inadvertently given us a unique memory for posterity. Because, hey, who else has a story like that from their wedding day?

Teena's family had gotten us a hotel room next to the river and across from the temple where we had just been married. After that long day, we were relieved and happy to excuse ourselves from my mom's "reception" and finally be alone.

We didn't have much money, so our first dinner as husband and wife was nothing fancy: a cheeseburger and sparkling apple cider. But it was the best meal ever because it was just the two of us together, now alone, finally married, finally alone together.

CHAPTER 21

Newlyweds

HONEYMOON

Teena's family had arranged for us to fly to Orlando, Florida, to have a honeymoon. We went to Walt Disney World and Universal Studios Theme Park. It was the first time for both of us, and we were excited.

Having no money, we found a store and bought a loaf of bread, peanut butter, and granola bars. This would be our breakfast, lunch, and dinner. But as always, Teena didn't seem to care at all, and we just enjoyed being in the sun and having this experience together.

While we were at Universal Studios, we became extremely thirsty. We didn't realize back then that you could ask for a cup of water at the park. Desperately needing a drink, we splurged and got a frozen lemonade. We sat on the park bench in the Central Park section of Universal Studios overlooking the lake. Soft classical music played in the background, and above was a perfectly clear blue sky with the sun sharing its warmth with us. We felt transported to another country, a magical place, the places I had only read about in books but never imagined seeing. We sat peacefully, quietly, alone in this little spot in the park while the music played gently in the background. I was just enjoying being with my special person. The moment was surreal, sitting there with the love of my life as if we were in another country sipping on frozen lemonade, a lifetime away from sleeping in the cold truck.

Teena took a sip of the frozen lemonade and then passed the drink back to me. I took a sip, trying not to take much as I wanted to make sure she had some too. The drink was a perfect combination of lemon and ice, perfect on a warm day. Then I set it on the ground, reached over to put my arm around Teena, and clumsily knocked the drink over with my foot. We looked at each other, and neither of us said much, but we both felt like weeping as it was much needed and there would be no more.

Teena began to be sick the second day we were there. She was in a lot of pain and for a day couldn't get out of bed. I didn't know it then, but it was the beginning of a hard road that we would endure together.

Our First Apartment

We decided to stay in Idaho Falls after we were married and finish my schooling there. Teena's health and the many medical tests she was undergoing prevented her from continuing school. Once we arrived home to what would be our first apartment (a one-bedroom that wasn't much to look at) in Idaho Falls, we got right to work, changing it into a home. The house was dark, with cigarette-smoke-stained walls. We painted it clean and bright, and Teena put up wallpaper. She decorated it beautifully. There was no air-conditioning, so the summer nights were hot and sweaty. We would laugh because we would lie in bed at night drenched in sweat and listen to the neighbors scream at each other.

Teena continued to experience the pain that had started on our honeymoon. We didn't have insurance, so she did her best to deal with it.

Every morning, Teena would take me to the bus so I could commute to school to ISU in Pocatello, fifty-one miles away. She was like a drunken sailor in the morning and would hit the curb on our way to the bus stop every morning in the exact same spot.

Teena worked that semester caring for handicapped children, finishing up at 10:00 p.m. each night. Her pain was getting worse. She felt that she had a urinary tract infection, so she kept going in to be tested, but tests always came back negative. Because of her condition, she would have to use the bathroom all day and all night.

I grew up in a house of boys and Teena in a house of girls, so I never learned proper bathroom etiquette. One night she fell in the toilet, not anticipating that the seat had been left up. It was kind of funny, but I never left the seat up after that.

CHAPTER 22

Breaking Free

O ne day, the phone rang out of the blue. We never got calls, so we were a bit surprised. I picked it up and heard Mom's voice.

"Chris, I have something important to ask you. I need you to give me a ride to work," she said. She continued, "You will have to drive up here about half an hour away, pick me up, and take me to work. And I need you to leave now."

I replied, "I'm sorry, Mom, I can't. I have to take Teena to work. It's over five miles away. That's too far for her to walk."

My mother replied, "She can walk. You need to make sure to take care of your parents and family."

I again replied, "No, I am not going to have her walk. It's wrong for you to even ask me that. Can't someone else who lives up there give you a ride?"

"No. You need to leave now and come and get me. Your wife can walk to work. It is your obligation as my son to help me get to where I need to go."

I again replied, "No, I can't do that. It's wrong of you to ask me to make Teena walk that distance, and I won't do it."

Mom continued, "I need you to leave now. If you don't, you are a failure as my son."

I stood my ground. She continued for a little while longer. I repeatedly said no. She kept badgering me, repeatedly telling me that I was a failure and I needed to take care of her. I stayed strong and kept refusing to give in to her manipulation.

Abruptly my mother lost her temper and told me, "Then you can just *f*** off!*" She hung up on me.

At that moment, a large amount of emotion welled up in me. Emotions that I had held back for more than two decades poured out. I began to sob, shedding profuse, real tears.

My wife was concerned. She held me, gave me words of encouragement, and thanked me for standing up to my mother. It was at this time that I realized I needed to break completely free of my mother and that I was in fact beginning to free myself from the hold she had on me. I also felt that I was finally starting to create a better life for myself, but Mom was trying to pull me back down. I would still respect her as my mother, but I could not let her interfere in our relationship, and I would not let her drag me down from reaching my dreams.

By the next semester, Teena and I were able to get an apartment at the Rocking J Apartments in Pocatello so we could be close to school. It was such a nice apartment for us. We had two bedrooms, and the heat was included, which Teena especially appreciated because she is always cold!

IDENTITY THEFT

Shortly after we moved to Pocatello, and shortly after Mom's toxic phone call in which she told me off, I wanted to apply for a credit card to begin to develop my credit rating. My parents had never really taught me about credit, but my wife had excellent credit and wanted to help me get mine started. So one day, she and I went into the bank branch and filled out the paperwork to apply for a credit/debit card and a checking account.

I told her, "I am super excited to get a credit card, as this is the first time I have ever applied for one."

After we had waited a little while at the bank for the outcome, the bank informed me that they couldn't issue me a credit card. They gave me a form that said I had "unpaid debts and had had a previous credit card relinquished." My wife and I were stunned. We didn't know what to say.

Teena looked at me, and I told her, "I have no idea what this is all about. I have never done anything like that."

The bank gave me a phone number to call to find out further details. When I spoke to the people on the phone, they told me, "You have opened various accounts including credit cards and lines of credit. You never paid your obligations and were sent to collections."

I was stunned and replied, "When did all this happen?"

They said, "Primarily between 1993 and 1994. There are some earlier negative accounts from the mid-1980s. You opened various accounts in Utah."

When I found out the dates, I learned that some of these predated my turning eighteen as I was only in my early teens in the mid-1980s, and many of the accounts were when I was in California on my mission.

I quickly figured out that Dad and Mom had used my Social Security number to open various accounts in my name, with Dad assuming my identity. As his name began with an *A*, he had used the name Chris A. Smith, A. C. Smith, or various combinations. My parents then did not pay their obligations. They had ruined my credit with their irresponsibility. I was devastated.

I broke down crying and then grew quite angered. I was so upset as I thought, *It wasn't enough that my parents raised me in homelessness, stole the money I earned working, and abandoned me at seventeen years of age. They went beyond that by trying to destroy any chance I had at a decent life by affecting my future financial prospects and ruining my credit rating.* Even though I was married and trying to create a new life for myself, the repercussions of their irresponsibility were still affecting me, and I had no idea how long this would last.

I spent the next year and a half, and many hours, trying to clear up my credit rating. I had to send several letters to various companies stating that I had been a victim of identity theft. This process felt interminable. It seemed that I was never getting anywhere and that the companies didn't believe me.

The entire time this was happening, my credit rating was ruined. I couldn't even open a checking account in my name. We had to do everything under my wife's name. Thankfully I had obtained a driver's license while I was in California, so I could prove that I was not living at the locations where the credit had been requested.

Eventually, after many long, long hours of calls and letters, I spoke to someone at the credit bureau to whom I could explain that my parents had done this while I was on a mission. She grew quiet and seemed to be touched. She said, "I am so sorry this happened to you. It is just wrong. I will take care of it."

After that, the items were all removed from my credit report, and I was able to move forward with my life.

I later found out that I was not the only child to whom my parents had done this. Several of my siblings had also had their identities stolen and credit rating ruined by my parents. From this point onward, whenever my parents came to visit, we would hide any checkbook or personal documents in a safe place to prevent further theft.

One day, Dad came and stayed the night at our house. We could hear him during the night rummaging through our drawers looking for something. I could only sadly assume he was looking for money, checks, or anything else he could use financially. That truly broke my heart.

THE FIRST OF MANY BAILS

Shortly after finding out my parents had stolen my identity and ruined my credit, I received a phone call late one night. I picked up the phone, and on the other end was Dad.

"Chris, this is your dad. I have been arrested, and I need you to come bail me out."

I responded, "I'm sorry, what did you say?"

My father repeated, "I have been arrested, and I need you to bail me out of jail."

"Arrested? Arrested for what?" I begged.

"I don't want to tell you, and it's not important. What is important is that I need you to come bail me out."

I was taken aback by this development, but I was not completely surprised. Dad's actions often were fraudulent. Growing up, I believe he had also taken advantage of his brothers and sisters (my aunts and uncles). I suspected he had probably been arrested for fraud of some sort. I also thought that it was quite brazen of him to steal my identity, ruin my credit and my future because of his greed, and then shortly thereafter ask me to bail him out of jail.

I replied, "Dad, I can't come up. I have a huge test tomorrow. Plus, we don't have any money to bail you out."

He continued to plead his case. "I really need you to come bail me out. I don't have any other options."

I said, "What about Johnny?" Johnny lived nearby and had become more established than I was as his wife had already finished school.

He replied, "John won't do it. I asked him, and he told me no. Mom won't do it either because she doesn't have any money. So I need you to do it. I need to get out of here so I can go back to work."

Back to work?! I thought. *Are you actually working?* He had not worked a steady job for years, more likely decades.

Eventually, I relented and agreed to bail Dad out. I drove the hour and a half to where he was in jail, in a small police station. I felt panic-stricken at the idea of walking into a police station because of how I had been raised. I breathed several times, attempting to quell the panic rising inside me, and eventually got up the nerve to go into the station.

When I walked in, I saw what appeared to be a clerk sitting at a desk at one end of the room. As I walked up to ask to see my father, I felt my heart pounding in my chest and my breathing quicken as a panic attack began to overwhelm me. The clerk was a large man, strong, broad-shouldered, a police officer, dressed in uniform, with a crew cut and a somewhat intimidating gaze.

I slowly stated the reason I was there. "Good evening, sir. I am here to see Mr. Smith. I believe he was arrested and is here somewhere."

The officer replied, "Who are you, and what is your relationship to Mr. Smith?"

Still panic-stricken, I told him my name and stated somewhat shakily, "He is my father. He asked me to come bail him out."

The officer noted my name, address, and relationship in the logbook and said, "Okay, son, come follow me."

We walked through a metal detector and proceeded to the back of the station. He led me to a small holding cell, maybe five by ten feet in size. In the holding cell, I saw Dad, dressed in an orange jumpsuit, sitting there with another man dressed in a shirt and tie.

The officer asked me, "Is this your father?"

I softly replied, "Yes."

At this point, the officer invited me to go in and talk to them in the holding cell.

The man in the tie introduced himself as a bail bondsman. He said, "Your father has been arrested and is trying to post bail. The amount is $500. Also, you would need to be willing to sign to guarantee that he will show up to his appointed court date. If he doesn't show up at the court date, you may be liable for additional costs and for us to find him."

I was shocked and dismayed at the amount of money. Five hundred dollars was a lot of money for a poor college couple both working at McDonald's making minimum wage. It was more than the budget for food for an entire month for us. We barely made enough money to live, not to mention we currently owed thousands of dollars in medical bills for Teena for the tests and treatments she was undergoing (for which there was still no diagnosis).

At this point, my father said, "Son, I know it's difficult for you, but I will pay you back. I promise. Can you please help me? I don't have anyone else."

I thought, *What about Mom? Shouldn't she be the one here? Why isn't she here?* I never found out if she had refused to bail him out or just couldn't afford it.

I told Dad, "You can't keep doing this! You need to just get a job and work like I do."

He replied, "I know, but my oil shale invention [apparently Dad had another revolutionary invention developing] is almost done, and I will hit it big. I promise I will pay you back for everything."

I knew it was an empty promise, like so many I had heard before. I was conflicted. I knew that I could not trust him, nor should I trust him. I also thought about the number of hours that Teena and I would have to work to make that money. Ultimately, since he looked so desperate and he was still able to manipulate me, I decided to help him.

I reluctantly agreed. "Okay, I will do it, but you need to promise me you will show up to your court date so I don't get stuck paying more." (It wasn't the first or last time I ended up paying for his bad choices).

He agreed and gave me his word that he would be there (for whatever that was worth). I pulled out the large sum of money and paid it to the bail bondsman. They completed the paperwork and released my father. Afterward, Dad thanked me.

Mom came to pick him up and never even spoke to me or thanked me. She didn't even get out of the car or roll the window down. She just casually waved at me, then made an obscene gesture with her middle finger to the police station as they drove off.

As they drove away, I thought, *Well, you're welcome. I guess Teena and I will be eating mac and cheese and ramen for the next month as I just spent our food budget on you. You can't even get out of the car or tell me thanks? I guess that's the norm. You both make stupid decisions rather than just doing what's right and working like normal people, and then you turn around and expect me to clean up your mess. I guess nothing has changed.*

I felt sad for my father. He had spent his life dreaming of making it big as a multimillionaire inventor, dreaming of a false reality he never made happen. Instead of just choosing a career and sticking with it, working, and doing the daily grind, he had followed an unrealistic dream. It had become an obsession for him. He had chosen to live like Captain Ahab, chasing the "white whale," ignoring the reality of what his "dream" had cost him, which was nearly everything. He was willing to exchange his ethics, his principles, his future, even his children's futures trying to find a shortcut to wealth. He could have chosen a much happier, less turbulent life by just choosing to work hard and do the right thing.

My parents' and subsequently their children's lives did not have to be so difficult. They *created* that life as a consequence of the small daily decisions they made, which if made differently, would have entirely changed the outcome.

I also wondered, *Why do I allow my parents to still manipulate me? Why do I feel the need to try to bail them out? Why do I not just let them deal with their own problems?* A child who is raised and conditioned to behave a certain way by an emotionally manipulative or abusive parent will find it very difficult to tell that parent "No!" and stand up to them.

I decided that I needed to create boundaries, to tell my parents "No!" and to let them deal with their problems they had caused. I needed boundaries to protect myself, but not only me but also to protect my wife and the future children I hoped to have. It would take me years and moving thousands of miles across the county before I would build those boundaries strong enough.

First Birthday as a Married Man

A few weeks later, it was my birthday. My wife had something special planned for us. A few days before my birthday, my mother called me and said that she wanted to throw a birthday party for me and that my siblings wanted to wish me a happy birthday. I replied I was busy in school and had a large test coming up, so I couldn't go. She insisted and kept stating how everyone missed me and wanted to see me.

I reluctantly agreed.

The day arrived, and we drove the hour and thirty to forty-five minutes to my parents' house for my "birthday party." When we arrived, we noticed a U-Haul moving van in the driveway. I immediately knew what was happening.

We got out of the car, and I found Mom lying in her bed complaining of a headache and drinking a Coke. She said, "Oh, how nice that you came. You can help us pack our truck because we are moving." She did not wish me a happy birthday or even recognize that fact as our reason for being there.

I asked where my siblings were, and she said that my sister Diana was crying in the bathroom, and my younger brother refused to help. Only one sibling was helping them load the truck.

Teena and I spent the next two to three hours loading the truck, and no one wished me happy birthday or asked how I was doing. We left after the truck was loaded.

On the way home, I further realized Mom's self-centered nature and vowed not to change my plans again to go to some occasion she had planned, even if she used my siblings as manipulation against me. I stayed up for several more hours, until 2:00 a.m., studying for my test. It was a "memorable" birthday.

CHAPTER 23

Creating a New Life

MONEY TROUBLES

After we moved to Pocatello and after bailing my father out of jail, Teena and I ran completely out of money. For the first several months, we ate from my in-laws' food storage. They had saved a large amount of food and other items to be used for an emergency—cheap, long-lasting items such as dried potatoes, rice, and wheat products. Teena and I were grateful for their preparedness and generosity.

For one or two months, we mostly ate Vienna sausages, Rice-A-Roni, and au gratin potatoes. In addition, my wife's uncle gave us a liver that he had obtained from hunting elk. So we ate liver and onions every night for dinner for five days straight. At the end of five days, it was starting to make me feel sick. I told Teena, "I don't think I can eat any more liver and onions. I don't think I ever want to eat them again—*ever!*" After that, we decided to stop eating liver and onions. (I have never eaten liver and onions again; even the thought of it makes me lose my appetite.)

After a few paychecks, we could afford to buy some groceries. We were (not surprisingly) very excited. We went to the discount grocery store near our house and found as many items we could on sale.

I held up some Rice-A-Roni and showed Teena. "What about this? They have several different flavors. We can eat a meal for just a little over a dollar."

She responded, "That sounds great. What do you think about macaroni and cheese with hot dogs?"

I said, "Sure, that sounds great, almost gourmet, like we are moving up from Vienna sausages!"

I also grabbed some tortillas, fruit, and vegetables. We decided that to have better nutrition, we also needed some dairy. I held up a gallon of milk and said, "We should get this. You need to drink milk to prevent osteoporosis."

Teena responded, "I am so excited to drink milk. I have really missed it. It's been a couple of months since I have drunk it."

We paid for our groceries and headed out of the store. Teena was ecstatic about our new food purchases, especially the milk. As soon as we got into the parking lot, she looked at me, smiled, and then began dancing spontaneously around the parking lot with the milk in her hands. It was fabulously fun. I refer to her dance as the "milk jug jig" to this day. Teena would often break into spontaneous dance and song throughout our marriage, something that caught me off guard the first few times but something that I absolutely love about her. We laughed heartily when she was done, and I smiled. I loved her more than ever, particularly after getting to know her spontaneity and her wonderful sense of humor.

CHEAP DATES AND THE GRIND OF LIFE

Because we had little money, our fun activities and dates would be going on long walks or hikes up into the mountains. One of our favorite activities was to feed the squirrels. When it was a beautiful sunny afternoon, we would walk around the neighborhood and head to the cemetery. Walking through the cemetery was a relaxing, quiet, pleasant stroll. It had beautiful tree-lined roads with no traffic and a wide pathway to walk on. It was safe and usually sunny. Often the trees were in bloom and the flowers were out, providing a sweet-smelling aroma that completed the perfect ambiance.

One sunny fall Sunday, with the leaves changing colors and a cool autumn scent in the air, we went for a walk to feed the squirrels. We brought along some bread and began to throw out pieces for them. At first, only a few squirrels would come up to us. As we proceeded to walk, within a short time, squirrels came from everywhere. We ended up with about thirty or forty squirrels walking around us and following us as we walked through the cemetery feeding them bread. We loved this activity because it was a cheap date, and we could bond with the environment, enjoy the sunshine, and enjoy each other's company. At the same time, we could feed the animals, have fun, and interact with nature.

I worked hard in college, taking eighteen credits each semester while working full time. I had straight A's, except in my speech class. I received an award for physics for earning the highest grade in all of the entry-level physics classes. I began to volunteer in Dr. Stephens's lab, doing scientific research on limb growth development. We would transplant limbs in chicken embryos, trying to elucidate the cascade of enzymes responsible for limb generation—in short, trying to grow chickens with three or four wings or legs. (I imagine that would be quite a boon for Kentucky Fried Chicken).

I also worked at McDonald's. My favorite spot was on the grill making sandwiches. I did not like working at the front counter because many customers were rude to me, acting as if I were beneath them because I worked at a fast-food restaurant. I remember a woman in particular who asked me, "Don't you want to do something more with your life? That is sad that you work at McDonald's."

Some of the most genuine, hardworking people I have ever met worked in the food service industry. I feel it is completely wrong to look down on someone because of what one may perceive as a "lesser job." To me, all honest work is good. It doesn't matter what we do, just that we work honestly and to the best of our ability.

OUR FIRST CHRISTMAS

Our first Christmas together, Teena and I didn't have money to buy any gifts. Teena's grandmother gave us a small plastic Christmas tree so we could have some decorations. In order to have some presents under the tree, we wrapped up things we already owned using the Sunday newspaper comics as wrapping paper that her grandmother would save and give us every time we visited her.

Teena joyfully placed the presents under our tree so we would have something to open on Christmas Day. The only gift we actually had that was new was a tin full of cookies that Teena's grandmother had sent us.

Because I had so many in my family, we each selected one sibling to whom we would give a gift. It saved us all money but ensured that each sibling would get a gift from another. We found out that we were to buy a present for my brother Darwin so we gave him the only gift we had to give at that time—our tin full of cookies.

When we went to the mall to look at all of the beautiful Christmas decorations, we decided to start a tradition. We walked into the Hallmark store and thought how wonderful it would be if we could buy one ornament each year that meant something to us as we reflected back on that year. Because we didn't have money and the ornaments were expensive, we decided we would come back the day after Christmas and choose one that was left over and on clearance. Our first ornament ended up being two mice sitting on a heart with a keyhole in the heart. The saying that we came up with to describe it was that "we had found the key to each other's heart."

We have continued that tradition of buying an ornament each year throughout our lives, with the idea that the ornament represents that year, and we have passed that tradition down to our children. It is fun to look back on the many ornaments from the different years and see the memories each one represents.

On that first Christmas Eve as a married couple, we heard a knock at the door. We opened the door and found a box of gifts left on our doorstep, which included pans and some other things we needed. We never found out who had given us the gifts, but we appreciated them greatly. We think it might have been from one of my older brothers and his wife who lived in the same city and were going to the same college.

FIRST INTERNSHIP

School continued in the spring semester with Teena and me working at McDonald's. I continued taking a large class load, eighteen semester hours, and working at my job as much as I was able.

The first spring we were married, I decided that I wanted to do an internship over the summer to improve my résumé and my experience. I found over a dozen summer internships, which included working at the Smithsonian and some other locations and universities, and I applied to all of them. As the spring rolled around at the end of the semester, each day I checked my mailbox to see if there was a chance I'd been accepted to any of these programs.

For a couple of weeks, I received a string of rejection letters. Each day, I continued to hopefully check the mailbox and excitedly open a letter from one of these programs, only to see the words "We thank you for your interest, but we are not accepting your application." Each day, I felt a little bit sadder and more dejected. I discussed it with Teena, and I tried to continue moving forward with hope. One more application remained, for which I had some hope that I would be accepted.

A few days later, on a beautiful sunny day, I came home to our apartment and opened our mailbox. Going through the mail, I saw a letter from Companion State University. I thought, *What is Companion State University? Did I apply to this program?*

As I opened the envelope, still standing at the mailbox, I saw it was a lovely letter from my wife that told me she was grateful for my attempts and my desire to get an internship, but instead of going away for the summer and being away from her, we could spend time together. When I was reading this letter, I looked up and saw she was standing in the doorway, quietly smiling and waiting to see my reaction. She could tell that I had been feeling a bit down from all the rejections, so she had written this note to lift my spirits.

After I read it, I smiled at her, walked over to her, gave her a hug and a kiss on her head, and told her, "You are the best. This means so much to me, and I love you." After that, I decided that it would be the *best* summer ever.

I always appreciated Teena for doing that kind deed. She was always looking out for me and trying to make my life better. I have not always been the best at showing my appreciation or acknowledgment of her, and I feel a bit sad about that as she has always tried to help me out.

CHAPTER 24

Growing Together

West Yellowstone

Prior to our marriage, my in-laws had moved to West Yellowstone, Montana, to open a sandwich shop with hopes of opening a Subway franchise. So instead of my taking a prestigious internship at a renowned institution (because I was rejected by all of them), we decided to spend the summer working in West Yellowstone, helping Teena's parents open a Subway sandwich shop.

After classes ended for the semester, we drove the three hours to West Yellowstone, Montana. When we arrived, we met my in-laws. They took us behind their sandwich shop and showed us our accommodations.

My mother-in-law excitedly exclaimed while pointing, "This trailer is from my parents. They are giving it to us to use. I used to go camping in this when I was a little girl! I have a lot of good memories of this trailer. We used to have so much fun with it."

Teena and I looked to where she was pointing and discovered our accommodations for the summer would consist of a small white camping trailer with yellow stripes, originally built in the fifties or sixties, about eight by twelve feet in size, parked behind the shop. It had seen better days, having sat for a couple of decades, uninhabited on the farm that belonged to my wife's grandparents. As they had used it when my mother-in-law was a child, it was far older than Teena or me.

As we entered it, Teena looked around and said, "This isn't so bad. I can hang some curtains up and make it look nice. I can also clean it up."

We went to work and cleaned up the trailer. I painted the top with some waterproof sealer so when it rained, it didn't "rain" inside as well. My mother-in-law made curtains, and my wife made it as homey as one could.

We enjoyed that small space together.

When you first walked through the door, to your right and at the front of the trailer was a small kitchen area. Straight ahead was the bathroom. The bathroom was quite a novelty because the shower and toilet were in the same two-feet-by-two-feet space, and you could sit on the toilet and shower at the same time. It was like multitasking! We had a few good laughs from that experience.

To the left was the booth table, to the right a closet, and at the end was a full-size bed. It was not much, but it was perfect for us, and we still look back fondly at our memories in the camping trailer that we turned into a home in West Yellowstone, Montana.

WE BUILT A SUBWAY SANDWICH SHOP

That summer, during the first month, I helped my father-in-law construct the Subway sandwich shop inside one of the local gas stations. We did everything including laying the tile. We worked long hours, most days from sunrise to sunset. After the shop was built, we had to learn to run it. For the first two weeks, I worked over one hundred hours each week learning from the district trainer about all the intricacies of running a Subway. We decided that I should be the one to learn it as I am a quick study and have a very strong constitution to be able to work those kinds of hours.

After I learned how to run the Subway shop, I spent the next month teaching my in-laws what I had learned. My mother-in-law had previously worked in a Subway so already knew quite a bit about it. That was the first time in my life I had worked more than one hundred hours in a week, but it certainly was not the last as those kinds of hours are normal for medical school and residency.

That summer, we also spent quite a bit of time exploring Yellowstone National Park and learning more about it. We visited all the major sites, swam in the Firehole River, and hiked many trails.

TEENA'S PAIN

The summer was a difficult one for Teena. The pain she had been experiencing since we were married, was getting much worse. Many times throughout that summer, she would sit in the hot shower and cry because of the pain. In those moments, I felt helpless and sad that there was nothing I could do to help her. She continued going to doctors, who would run urinalysis and then tell her that there was nothing wrong with her. Ultimately, she found a primary care doctor who was willing to refer her to see a specialist.

Teena had been struggling with pain and other symptoms for some time, which had begun shortly after we were married. The general practitioners she went to could never figure out what was wrong and generally just treated her as if she must be crazy or malingering. She finally found a doctor who referred her to a specialist. We went to this specialist with great hope that he would know what was wrong and be able to treat her.

Once the doctor came into the examination room, he had his staff prep Teena so that he could use a scope to see inside her bladder. The doctor could clearly see her problem: her immune system had been attacking her own body. The protective lining of her bladder was damaged; there were holes in the lining, causing the bladder to harden and shrink, consequently causing nerve damage and constant inflammation, which was triggering great pain.

We were relieved to finally have a diagnosis, but we didn't expect what would come next. He told us that there was no cure. He gave my wife a pamphlet about how to live with this illness and began to go over palliative treatment options.

We left the doctor's office and began a long two-hour drive back to Teena's parents in West Yellowstone. She wept the entire way, trying to come to terms with the idea that she might always have to battle this pain and live in constant agony. I could do little to console her, so I just listened in silence as she wept and occasionally muttered words that I can't even recall. I just felt powerless and helpless. I wanted to do anything to ease her pain. I would have even traded places with her and taken the pain on myself. The most I could do was hold her hand and pray that she would find some measure of relief.

Teena's Treatment

The day quickly arrived for Teena to begin her treatments. We arrived at the clinic for the first of many treatments that Teena would receive over the next few years. After we checked in at the clinic, the nurse led us to the back of the office and directed us to a treatment room. We sat quietly in the room as we waited for Dr. Tall to come in. He entered the room and began to explain, "This may be quite painful for you as you have so much inflammation and so many glomerulations [holes] in the bladder that have gone untreated for many years. I am hopeful that in time this will give you some relief."

Teena looked over at me apprehensively, and I grabbed her hand to try to support her during the procedure. As soon as the doctor began, Teena tightly squeezed my hand as she was in excruciating pain. Because she had gone untreated for so long, her pain was intolerable. I held her hand because that was all I could do.

The day was long and hard, and during the night, I awoke and found Teena wasn't in bed. Worried, I looked around the house for her and found her in the tub, crying in pain as she sat in the hot water, trying to make it better. My soul ached for her, and I wanted to just take away her pain. I told her, "I am so sorry you have to go through this. I wish I could do something to help you." I could not do anything but just hold her and try to comfort her. I felt powerless and helpless.

We kept going back for treatments, each time with a similar outcome, and the relief Teena desperately needed just didn't seem to come. She began to become depressed. Sleeping was hard; sitting was hard; life was hard. From her earliest thoughts, my dear wife had wanted to be a mother. Not only could she not be a mother, but she wondered how she could just get through today to get through tomorrow.

At the time, I was taking eighteen credit hours, trying to hammer out my education. I would work extra by tutoring students and study the rest of the time. There was little more I could do about our situation. It was hard, but they were still some of the best days of our early life together. We could not bypass the problem; we could only go through it and try to make the best of it.

Teena said she felt useless, "like a blob just taking up air and space." Regardless, she always had a good meal prepared for me and a nice, clean home to come to. That was so much more than I'd had before I had her in my life.

Sometime later, on the evening of our first anniversary, I walked into the house. I could hear music playing in the background and followed it to find Teena out on the back patio. There was a table nicely set with china, which had been Teena's grandmother's. It was accompanied by a nice white tablecloth, with flickering candles completing the romantic scene. Teena greeted me with a smile, and we sat down to eat lasagna, salad, and garlic bread. She knew it was my favorite. Never before had someone taken such efforts to make me feel so loved and important.

As we ate, *The Lawrence Welk Show* played softly in the background. The show was playing dance and big band music from the fifties. It completed the perfect romantic scene Teena had envisioned, as if we were eating in a fancy restaurant with live music.

Teena grabbed my hands and asked me, "Come dance with me, love."

I quickly responded, "I would love to, but you'll have to lead as I'm not a very good dancer."

In the candlelit room, I held her tightly against me, her small hand in mine, and we danced. As we slowly moved to the music, I felt loved, loved more than I had in my entire life. I felt secure. I felt so happy. I felt so complete. I felt that everything would be alright.

This was something Teena would continue to do throughout our marriage: a meal and a dance. She loves to dance. Her grandparents were dancers. Her dad danced, and he had taught her from the time she was a baby. Dancing became something we did when I came home. Turn on the music, hold her, and dance. It was one of the things I could do to bring her joy. I didn't know a thing about dancing, but it didn't matter to her. Although she could waltz and do all other forms of dance, she was content to just sway back and forth or dance a simple waltz that she taught me: one, two, three—one, two, three—slow, quick, quick—slow, quick, quick. And we danced right there in the kitchen.

Teena's treatments were getting a little better, but we still did not see the improvement that we were hoping for. It was hard. The medical bills were adding up, and all we could do was pay five dollars here and a couple hundred there. It was two steps forward and five steps back.

The doctor wanted to perform surgery. However, we just could not come up with the thousands it would take. We were unable to secure insurance for Teena because of her preexisting illness. It seemed just impossible. At the time, there were few treatment options, so we just kept moving forward, doing the best we could. I was getting close to completing my undergraduate degree, so all we could do was look forward and hope that God would provide a way. Medical school was in our future, and somehow I knew it would all work out.

CONTINUED TREATMENTS AND HAIR FALLING OUT

Finally, we went one day for Teena's treatment, and the doctor informed us that the FDA had just approved a new treatment option. We were so hopeful. This was great!

It was great until we found out how expensive the medication was and its side effects. The medication was at least 20 percent of our monthly budget. Nevertheless, we did what we had to do, and she started the new medication.

In the beginning, the medication would make Teena feel nauseated, and then her hair started to fall out. I wondered, *Is this going to be worth it?* The more time passed, the more Teena became upset about losing her hair. Every time it would clump out, she would cry.

A dear friend who had gone through radiation treatment and lost her hair told Teena, "Just shave it off and you will feel better."

One day, I came home from school, and Teena met me in the doorway with the clippers she used to cut my hair and told me, "Just cut it off so I can be done with it."

I felt panicked. "Are you sure? We can't undo this."

She insisted she was prepared and certain. So she sat there, and I shaved her thinning head of hair. As the shaved hair slowly fell to the ground, my determination to try to make things better was intensified. After that, Teena never cried another time about losing her hair. She was beautiful even when she was bald. I had fallen in love with her, not her hair. She wore scarves, hats, whatever, and didn't worry another day about the hair that was clogging up the drain and falling on the keyboard as she typed. She was beautiful even when she was bald.

After a couple of months, the treatment began to work. Her pain was getting better. Her symptoms were lessening. Overall, we were finally seeing success! Finally, some relief.

GRAMPS

In these college days when my wife was sick, we had found a job living with an elderly man and taking care of him in exchange for rent and a monthly sum of money. This was very helpful for us as Teena, who was still sick every day, could stay at the house and help the elderly gentleman as best she could. Everyone called him "Gramps." On school days, I would help her when I got home.

We lived with Gramps until he passed away. After he passed, we found the cheapest apartment we could get. It was a basement apartment beneath a house, where the ceiling was only six feet high. I spent most of the time slightly stooped so I wouldn't scrape my head on the ceiling. In addition, there was only one bedroom, and the bathroom was off the bedroom. The bedroom was so small that our bed filled it. In order to get to the bathroom, you had to crawl across the bed. It became very awkward if we had any guests over and they needed to use the bathroom. This apartment was not fancy, but it served the purpose of getting through the rest of college until we moved for medical school.

On Sundays, Teena would make treats, and we would take them to some of the single elderly people in our area. Every Wednesday, we taught handicapped children. Teena had a way with handicapped children and adults. I always admired how she jumped right in and lovingly interacted with people who had special needs when others tended to awkwardly avoid them.

TRIO Tutoring

I had worked at McDonald's during my first year of college. Teena had ended up working at McDonald's with me. She'd had a good job working as a developmental therapist for developmentally delayed people or people with mental illnesses, such as schizophrenia. She enjoyed this job helping people. But one day her boss approached Teena and said she needed to change her billing practices. In essence, he wanted her to bill for services she wasn't doing to bring the company greater profits. Teena felt that this was just plain wrong. So rather than be dishonest, she quit that job and came to work with me at McDonald's. It was quite a step-down, but at least it was honest work.

While I worked at McDonald's, I was looking for a better job. I saw a tutoring position advertised by TRIO student services. I applied and was accepted. I made a little more money than McDonald's, but more importantly, I really enjoyed the work.

TRIO is a student services organization that provides free tutoring and other services to disadvantaged and nontraditional students. As school was my forte, this fit me very well. We received training on teaching methods and how to help these students be successful. I tutored in biology and chemistry. Some of my student clients were mothers returning to school after a prolonged absence or those with learning disabilities. I would meet with them two to three times a week and go over their assignments with them. I would help them study and learn the material using different strategies to help them retain the material, such as mnemonics and word association. I found great satisfaction in helping these students as traditional methods often failed them.

One person I really looked up to in the TRIO program was the tutoring supervisor, Will. Will was a fellow college student a couple of years ahead of me. He was born with cerebral palsy that had left him paralyzed on one side of his body, which of course made his life very difficult. Nonetheless, he insisted on walking with canes rather than using a wheelchair.

In addition, he had some partial contracture of the right arm and leg because of the paralysis. However, he did not let that hold him back. He had graduated high school with honors and was studying a scientific discipline. Furthermore, he had actually served a two-year mission as I had. Additionally, he was in charge of the tutoring program. He always carried a positive "can do" attitude and never gave up trying. He also never gave up on anyone. He was an inspiration to me in how positive and upbeat he was. He was amazing in his ability to persist and overcome his problems to be a success. He was also a fabulous tutor at helping those with learning disabilities to learn. He is one of my heroes and one of the most inspirational people I have had the privilege of knowing.

DOGSLED

Teena and I visited her parents in West Yellowstone over our second Christmas break together. They get a lot of snow there in the winter. In fact, they had so much snow, it was up to the roof. In order to get the snow off so it didn't collapse, my father-in-law drove his snowblower onto the roof and blew the snow off. My in-laws had also made a snow tunnel they could walk through to get from their house to the restaurant they owned. I had never seen so much snow. I felt as if I were in the Arctic or on some ice-covered planet from a sci-fi movie.

Teena's dad also arranged for us to ride a snow track van into the park. These are large vans with tank treads instead of wheels that are used in heavy snow, those same vehicles you see in documentaries that scientists use to study polar bears in Alaska. Yellowstone Park was beautiful in the winter, completely white, nearly devoid of humanity, with mist and steam rising from geysers like tendrils into the sky. It really was a sight to behold.

That winter, I also had the opportunity to drive a dogsled team. There were two teams. The dogsled owner would drive one, and he asked if I wanted to drive the other team. I gladly jumped at such a once-in-a-lifetime opportunity and jubilantly responded in the affirmative. Teena rode the sled while I drove it. I yelled, "Mush!" and the dogs bolted into a run. I was amazed at how strong the dogs were and how effortlessly they ran.

We glided over the snow, making a comforting crunching sound. I followed the dogsled owner as we wound through the woods at Island Park just outside Yellowstone. I marveled at how the dogs functioned as a team, following the lead dog perfectly in unison without missing a step. They ran continuously without seeming to be fatigued.

Eventually, we reached the point where we needed to turn around. It was a narrow point in the trail. I quickly found out a team of sled dogs is not easy to turn, but they will follow the lead dog if that dog changes course. So the owner grabbed the lead dog's collar and led it to turn the team around. Once he was able to redirect the lead dog, the other dogs quickly followed in unison. I marveled at the leadership of this alpha dog and how well the other dogs followed it.

As we rode back home, I pondered the experience. I reflected on how this had been a metaphor for life. At times we will have a leader whom we follow, and as long as the team works in unison with everyone contributing, much can be accomplished. Additionally, sometimes a new direction is needed for the team or for us individually. Oftentimes that change in direction takes quite a bit of effort, and sometimes we need an external guide. Whether that is a trusted mentor, the universe, or God, that guide can put us back on our path. Once we start down the new path and continue to move forward, especially as a team with others, we can accomplish much good.

I also thought how much easier it was to keep moving forward in the snow rather than be stagnant. I noticed that when we moved forward on the sled, we hardly sunk into the snow. However, when we stopped moving and sat in place, the sled would sink, and it became more difficult to move forward again. I think this is like life: when we are moving forward towards a goal, it is easier to keep moving, but when we stop and are stagnant, it becomes more difficult to begin moving forward again as we are stuck in the process.

CHAPTER 25

Application and Acceptance

APPLYING TO MEDICAL SCHOOL

At the end of my undergraduate studies, I was trying to decide what to do with my life. I had been majoring in Zoology to that point, but was considering switching to a Chemistry major. I scheduled a meeting with Dr. Gardner of the chemistry department to discuss the potential of doing a combined MS/BS program. I went to the office and met with Dr. Gardner, who was one of my organic chemistry professors. She was someone I thoroughly admired and whose opinion I trusted. She welcomed me in and began to discuss the MS/BS program. She told me all the details and said that I would be a good candidate should I choose to apply.

Basically, it would require me to change my undergraduate major to chemistry and finish out that program while at the same time starting the master's program in chemistry. The idea of earning dual degrees was intriguing to me.

Dr. Gardner then asked me, "What are you thinking about doing with your life?"

I told her, "I'm considering applying to medical school and becoming a physician if I can get in."

At that point, she told me, "I think that you should just move forward and apply to medical school and not waste time with a master's degree.

Medical school takes a long time, and the more quickly you can get through it, the better."

I went home and spoke with Teena, and we decided I would apply to medical school.

One of the most critical parts of applying to medical school is taking the Medical College Admission Test, the MCAT. The test is not for the faint of heart. Per the Association of American Medical Colleges (AAMC):

> The Medical College Admission Test® (MCAT®) is a standardized, multiple-choice, computer-based test that has been a part of the medical school admissions process for more than 90 years. Each year, more than 85,000 students sit for the exam. The MCAT exam tests examinees on the skills and knowledge that medical educators, physicians, medical students, and residents have identified as key prerequisites for success in medical school and practicing medicine. The content is divided into four sections: 1) Biological and Biochemical Foundations of Living Systems, 2) Chemical and Physical Foundations of Biological Systems, 3) Psychological, Social, and Biological Foundations of Behavior, 4) Critical Analysis and Reasoning Skills.

The year I applied to medical school, there were approximately 47,000 applicants for 17,000 positions nationwide. For the University of Utah, acceptance rates were around 4.6 percent.

When I studied for the MCAT, I didn't have money to complete a test prep course, so I prepared as I had in the past. I went back to my "safe space" and "my home away from home": the library. I checked out every book on the MCAT and read them all. I completed every practice test I could find, answering thousands of questions. I did this while working full-time and taking eighteen credits a semester. Needless to say, I slept only four to five hours most nights. It was a cheap way to prepare, but it was the only way I could do it. I spent several months straight doing this, taking a break from studying only on Sundays, when I would spend time with Teena.

The day of the MCAT came, and I was actually sick with a pretty severe upper respiratory infection, severe allergies, and a sinus headache. But I could not reschedule the test because I did not have the time or money to do so. So I took some cold medicine to try to dry out my secretions as much as possible and to relieve my headache partially. I was not very excited to take the test, and I was afraid I would fail because of my condition. But as I had done with bungee jumping before, I leaned forward, let go, and hoped for the best.

Surprisingly, I actually did quite well, scoring well above average, in the top 5 percent of national test-takers. It was much better than I would have even imagined doing. I guess reading and studying books from the library is still a good way to prepare.

Ironically, before the test, I was sitting at a table, waiting for it to start. Some of the other students who were also taking the test gathered around the table. One of them was an obnoxious, arrogant guy who loudly proclaimed he was going to "rock the exam" and go to med school while some of the other students would not because he was part of the "superior gene pool" and the rest of us were in the "shallow end." I'd had a few other classes with this guy, and he was always obnoxious and arrogant. He never knew that I always beat him for better grades in the classes. I did much better than him on the MCAT. I was accepted to medical school and he was not, probably due to his extreme arrogance. I am glad he was not going to be a physician.

When I applied to medical school, I figured I would hedge my bets and apply to a number of places across the country. I had no pretense that I was going to be accepted. I only hoped that maybe one of them would give me a chance. Again, "I leaned forward and leapt," fearful of the consequences but hoping for the best.

There was no internet by which one could do an electronic application, nor were there fillable PDFs. Teena and I completed the applications old school, with a typewriter. I could not have done it without my wife. She helped me fill out all those applications on an old typewriter we had borrowed. The process was long and laborious with no room for error. If we did make an error, we had to use Wite-Out and erase the mistake as best we could. Each application had a separate charge, which added up to several hundred dollars, nearing a thousand. That was a large sum of money for a couple who worked at McDonald's and tutored. That was the initial cost, not even approaching the amount we would have to spend to travel to all of these universities for interviews.

My first interview was at the University of Utah School of Medicine. We did that one first because it was within driving distance. I did not want to go alone, so Teena and I made the four-to-five-hour drive down to Salt Lake City. On the way there, we talked about the hope of my getting accepted to medical school and how exciting that would be.

My first interview at the University of Utah was with Dr. Judd, who was the dean of students. On my application, I had briefly mentioned being homeless as a teenager. I wondered if I would be asked to explain that in detail. But Dr. Judd never brought it up, asking me typical interview questions such as "What are your strengths and weaknesses?", "Why do you want to go to medical school?", and "Why would you make a good physician?"

In the interview, she explained that "typically if you were to get a letter within two weeks after the interview, that would be a rejection letter. The acceptance letters usually come much later after we have interviewed all the applicants, and this is only the beginning of the interview season."

She also explained that an early acceptance to the medical school was extremely rare. There were a large number of applicants for the one hundred positions with the aforementioned acceptance rate. I completed that interview and did several others that day. Teena and I then drove home to Pocatello, Idaho.

Two weeks passed rather quickly, and one afternoon, I came home and saw a letter from the University of Utah School of Medicine in the mailbox. I was crestfallen as I thought, *Oh no, this is my rejection letter,* because Dr. Judd had said that only rejection letters came out two weeks after the interview. I had flashbacks to all those rejection letters I had received that prior summer.

I told myself, *Wow, I must have done quite poorly in the interview, or I was just not that competitive based on my grades.* That familiar, negative voice in my head came back. I told myself that there was no way I would have received an early acceptance. I was quite sad and felt heavy, and I was afraid to tell Teena. So rather than open the letter inside the house and have her see my failure once again, I slowly peeled the envelope back while standing in the driveway, expecting to see the words "We regret to inform you . . ."

I nearly keeled over with surprise when instead I read the words "We are pleased to inform you that you have been accepted into the University of Utah School of Medicine, class of 2001."

I stood in shock, staring at the letter, not believing it was real at first. I looked through the document further to confirm it was not a prank and made sure the signature on the bottom was legitimate. It was signed by Dr. Judd, who had interviewed me.

Teena saw me standing in the driveway reading the mail and was concerned, so she came outside to check on me. She asked me, "Are you okay? Is that a rejection letter from the U of U?"

I looked up from the letter nearly breathless and said, "No, it's actually an early acceptance letter to Utah. I'm going to be a medical student!"

It took a moment for that to sink in with her. She then squealed in delight, ran over, and gave me a kiss and a hug. I was still reeling at the thought of getting an early acceptance. Still in disbelief, I read through the letter multiple times to make sure I had not misread or misinterpreted it. Each time I read it, the letter still said the same thing, that I had been accepted into medical school. I was awed, knowing that I had not done this by myself. I felt that this was Divine intervention for us. Because of our limited finances, we didn't know how we were going to pay for flights and hotels for me to interview at any of the other places. This early acceptance had made it so that instead of spending money interviewing at remote locations, we could instead use our meager resources to relocate to Salt Lake City. I felt it truly was a miracle.

I immediately wrote to the U of U School of Medicine and confirmed my acceptance. My wife and I were extremely excited and glad, and we wanted to share the news with people we knew, people we thought cared about us and would be excited to hear the news.

I called up my parents. Mom answered the phone. I excitedly told her, "Great news! I was just accepted into medical school, and you will someday have a doctor for a son."

She bluntly replied, "Well, don't screw this up."

I was stunned. She did not say "Congratulations," "Good job," or anything positive. She just acted as if I were a total screwup who would amount to nothing. I was rather shocked at her response. She had always acted as if I were inadequate and had never accomplished anything, that what I did was never enough, that I would always fail.

The reality was that I was graduating with my bachelor's degree in just over three years' time and with high honors (summa cum laude) from ISU. Following Mom's response to my excitement, I decided that, for the most part, in the future I was not going to share any more good news with her because she viewed everything I did in a negative light. Furthermore, I felt that no matter what I accomplished or what accolades I received would never be enough for her—not because of my inadequacy but because of her insecurities.

Dad was more positive and was excited. He told me, "Great job! I'm proud of you!" I think Dad believing in me and thinking I could succeed had given me the confidence to try. Despite his weaknesses and flaws, one thing my father did very well was to encourage us to try and also to believe in us.

The Summer before Medical School

The summer before I started medical school, we went to Montana to visit Teena's family. When we got there, Teena discovered that her baby sister, Ange, had been recommended for special education for the upcoming school year. Ange had just completed Kindergarten and the school had written a letter about how she was a "problem child" because she didn't know her alphabet, drew letters the wrong direction, and hadn't lost her teeth. Teena was furious. Although she was fifteen years older than Ange, Teena was very close to that little girl. She had always helped take care of her when she was a baby and took her places all the time. Teena felt adamant that there was nothing wrong with Ange, but rather the problem was the school in the small Montana town, where many of the graduates were illiterate.

When it came time for us to go home, Teena brought Ange with us. She began right away teaching her sister the alphabet, phonetics, and how to read. That's how she spent her summer. Her sister was her next quest.

By the end of summer, Ange was reading just fine. We took her back to West Yellowstone, and Teena wanted to make sure she was put in the regular class and that the school knew she was on track. In fact, Ange had actually surpassed the benchmarks the school had set. Nevertheless, the school was offended that Teena had taught Ange better than they had; she had accomplished in one summer what they couldn't accomplish in a school year. The school continued to label Ange, so Teena couldn't bear to leave her sister with these people who had found offense at her accomplishments rather than happiness in her success. This began the long road of raising Teena's sister until she graduated high school. Ange became a daughter to me as we cared for her as our own.

My college years were challenging in many respects but ended well. Johnny's wife had their first baby, and we went to see them in the hospital. Teena held that tiny baby and then cried all the way home because she had beheld that little miracle, she so yearned for but knew she might never have. As well, Teena's treatments had been hard and initially not very successful. We had also experienced many other events: Teena had lost her hair, I had moved my parents three times and bailed Dad out of jail, Gramps had died and with him had gone our housing and income, and Teena's medical bills were in the thousands now.

However, by the end of my college experience, a new treatment for Teena's condition had been released, and even better, it was working. Teena wasn't depressed anymore. Furthermore, the doctor—having learned of our plight and my acceptance to medical school—wanted to help us, so he wrote off Teena's medical bills. We were finishing up in Idaho, I was finished with my undergraduate studies, and we were moving on to another chapter in our lives. God had blessed us greatly.

CHAPTER 26

Medical School Begins

SELF-DOUBT

Most medical schools start by having a "white coat ceremony," wherein medical students are welcomed to the medical community and given their first white coat while reciting the Hippocratic oath. The day of the ceremony arrived. By this time, we had moved down to Salt Lake City into the University Village student housing. The ceremony was held at Kingsbury Hall, a large, beautiful concert hall, with classical paintings on the wall and a mezzanine level. As I sat with my class waiting for the ceremony to start, I looked around at the surroundings. I felt a bit out of place as I had never imagined I would be in a place like this, much less starting medical school.

My thoughts started to run away from me as I sat quietly waiting for my name to be called. What if Mom was right? What if I was a screwup? Could I do this? Could I actually go to med school and become a physician?

Physician? Doctor? MD? Failure . . . screwup . . . never good enough . . .

The words bounced around in my head as self-doubt crept in. Those words that I had heard from my mother most of my life began to pound in my mind as I felt my pulse and breathing rise. Panic began to set in.

What about my scars, emotional and physical? What if I am too weak, too tired, too dumb? What if I fail again?

I was scared. I didn't know if I could do it. What if I could not? I was worried. Then I remembered Teena's smiling face and her pride when I'd showed her the acceptance letter. I remembered my time sleeping in the truck, promising that I would learn to endure things I imagined I could not endure, to learn to become exhausted striving for those things that are beyond my grasp.

I knew I could possibly fail, but I remembered the lesson I had learned from bungee jumping: Sometimes you just have to lean forward and let go, hope for the best, and fall toward the unknown, trusting in yourself and those whom you love. Just as with bungee jumping, you may fall a little, but you will rise again, and it will be one amazing ride.

I looked around the room and met my wife's beautiful eyes as she smiled at me, comforting me like a tender caress to my soul. Her smile chased away the negative shadows of my past, and her smile seemed to say, *You've got this. You can do this. I believe in you.*

I smiled in my heart as I heard my name called. "Christopher L. Smith, come forward to get your white coat."

I took a step forward. All those negative demons of my past vanished.

Once I went forward, the fear disappeared. I had embraced that fear and walked through it. I learned another truth that day, a lasting truth that you cannot be beaten by something you don't fear. I embraced who I was, embraced my fear, and believed in myself. All that was left was my will to succeed and those good people in my life who loved me and accepted me.

I took a deep breath, I walked forward, and I accepted my first white coat, the white coat of a medical student, someday in the future to be exchanged for the white coat of a physician. I was officially a medical student. The words seemed foreign to me yet familiar, as if this were something to which I had been guided to be, a role that my scars had strengthened me to become.

Looking at my wife in the audience, I knew we could do it together. I knew I was not alone. When we feel we are alone, we are at the mercy of the storm. But when we are not alone, we draw in strength and are not as fragile.

When I saw Teena's smile, I felt her support. I knew that together we would stand against whatever storms we would face in the future.

MEDICAL SCHOOL

Medical school is intense. The first two years are similar to college, just more rigorous with learning information much more quickly. It has been described as "drinking from a fire hose." One takes the equivalent of twenty-six to twenty-eight credit hours per semester. I studied very hard. I would often live in the medical school library when I needed to study. Before medical school even started, I set a goal of not studying on Sundays. I wanted to dedicate one day to God and also spend time with my wife. It was important to me to maintain those relationships and keep them a top priority in my busy life. Some Sundays, I did have to be at the hospital, but if I was not required to be there, I was at church or at home. Sometimes this goal meant that I slept only a few hours before Monday so that I could get up early and study. However, Sundays were by far my favorite day of the week in medical school.

The first semester, I had gross anatomy. Every physician remembers gross anatomy and in particular the peculiarly strong smell of the form-aldehyde. We immersed ourselves so much in the anatomy lab that our clothes and skin would become saturated with the smell of formaldehyde. When I came home from school, I had to immediately change my clothes, and Teena made me leave them outside. I threw a couple of outfits away after the class because the smell permeated them so much. The smell was so strong that it could not be washed out no matter how many times you tried. Even the anatomy textbooks smelled like the anatomy lab. Walking around the medical school campus, you can tell who the first-year students are because the smell of the cadaver lab lingers on them.

I had a couple of study partners for gross anatomy, and we spent a lot of time studying. After hours, we went to the anatomy cadaver lab to practice learning the anatomic structures such as muscles, nerves, arteries, and veins. Often, I would be in the lab studying with my classmates, and slowly the sun would set, the lab getting a little darker. Sometimes it would get a bit surreal being surrounded by cadavers as the room slowly darkened . . . *I could imagine a horror movie starting like this*, I said to myself . . . but it was great learning. One of the other classes during the first years of medical school is a clinical skills class. In that class, you learn the basics of physical examination and other skills. One afternoon, I sat down by my friend Denton Roberts in the clinical lab, surrounded by microscopes and other items. We had found out that this day we were going to learn to draw blood, and we were going to practice on each other.

Denton and I sat across from each other and looked down at the materials in front of us. There were several vacuum red-cap bottles and needles in front of us. Our instructor explained, "Today you are going to draw blood and learn how to do it on each other. Part of the reason is so that you will gain empathy for your patients on whom you will be ordering these tests."

Denton and I looked at each other and made that *uh-oh* face.

The instructor proceeded to explain in detail the method of accessing veins and drawing blood. We put on our latex gloves, picked up the needles and vacuum tubes, and looked at them. I wondered, *Can I really do this?*

Denton and I played Rock, Paper, Scissors to determine who would go first. I won, so I went first. I placed a tourniquet around Denton's bicep, then I felt around in his antecubital fossa, between the upper arm and forearm, feeling for a vein. After what seemed an eternity, I found a tubular structure that felt kind of like a worm and decided that was likely the vein. I hesitantly inched the needle with the tube toward his arm. I trembled a bit. As I approached his vein, I told myself, *You can do this. You have done hard things before*, and I steadied my shaking hand. I pierced Denton's skin with the needle and felt it puncture his vein. Blood began to fill the vacuum tube.

I removed the needle and looked up at Denton, and he said, "Now it's my turn, I guess." He placed the tourniquet on my arm, and I felt the tightness. As he approached my arm, I tensed, waiting for the stick. I felt the sharp prick of the needle and winced at the pain. On the first pass, he didn't get any blood. He tried again, and still no blood. After a few tries, the blood began to flow into the tube. I held pressure on it afterward and later developed a large bruise in my arm.

Later, as the year progressed and people heard about my goal of not studying on Sundays, they expressed that I was crazy, would do poorly in my classes, and would probably flunk out of school. But all through medical school, I kept this promise to myself. I know that I learned the information better and retained it better. I found that when you put God first, He makes up the difference. I know God magnified my ability to retain what I studied in a shorter time because I gave Him my time for that day once a week. Furthermore, having the downtime to focus on other things, especially family, allowed my mind to relax and let me learn more easily and have better mental health. This day off kept my priorities in line rather than making medical training all-consuming. I feel it is important that in any endeavor, we try to maintain balance among our personal relationships, professional work, and spiritual relationships, whatever spirituality we believe in.

Interestingly, by the end of medical school, I graduated in the top ten in my class with high honors and was inducted into the prestigious medical honor society Alpha Omega Alpha (more on this later).

PSYCHIATRY

Psychiatry was intriguing for me to study as I developed a deeper self-awareness. As we studied different disorders, including anxiety, PTSD, and depression, I started to see shades of these disorders in myself. I began to understand the anxiety and baggage I was carrying from when I was growing up.

I have often struggled with anxiety. My brain is continually analyzing everything, including scanning and planning for potential threats. I usually have backup plans for the backup plans for almost everything, which I develop nearly subconsciously. I believe this is due to my early life, always expecting the worst to happen. As a result, I consistently had anxiety about failing, about not being good enough, about everything falling apart.

PROGRAMMING A COMPUTER

The summer after my first year of medical school, I arranged to work on a project with Dr. Ash, the pathology professor. His goal was ambitious: to write a computer program to show slides and help students practice. I was not a programmer, having taken only a rudimentary computer programming course in high school. However, I accepted the challenge.

I spent the next three months learning a programming system. At the end of the summer, I was able to present to Dr. Ash a fully functioning computer program, and he was able to use it to help students study. The program would randomly show students slides of different cells, and they would have a multiple-choice question to identify the type of tissue. I was quite proud that in three months, I had been able to take his esoteric idea and write a fully functioning program without any training in computer programming.

SECOND YEAR OF MEDICAL SCHOOL

Early in the fall of the next school year, I arrived for one of my second-year medical school lectures a little late. When I arrived, I noticed that a lot of my classmates were crying. *Well, what's going on?* I wondered.

Shuffling in, I quickly found my seat. A professor I didn't know stood up, introduced himself as a counselor, and announced that he was there to deliver bad news. He then explained that one of my classmates had been killed by her husband the previous night in a domestic violence assault. The news stunned everybody in the class.

We had received a swift reality check to the cocoon of medical school by a striking example of man's inhumanity to man, which in later years of our training we would see far too often. What made this sad news all the sadder was that the murdered woman was one of the kindest, nicest, gentlest people I knew. She had spent time in the Peace Corps, among other good works. We had a memorial for her, and she is remembered by my class to this day.

I did well the first two years of medical school. I was able to earn honors in most of my courses. Medical school was graded as honors, pass, or fail. When I studied, I fully embraced the coursework. I would usually overstudy and memorize most of the information. School and learning had always been the bedrock of my soul. I have always found school to be a safe space. For most of my life, it was one of the few constant foundations I had.

CHAPTER 27

Adoption

A few years after we were married, Teena and I decided to have children. For several years, we had tried to conceive but were unsuccessful. During my second year of medical school, we visited a fertility doctor. We met with the medical team multiple times and underwent many tests, but they could not find a cause for the infertility. We entered every appointment hopeful that they might have found a reason and thereby a potential treatment. At every appointment, we were crestfallen to learn that they still did not have an answer for us.

We tried many different types of fertility treatments, including multiple medications. Each month, my wife would remain hopeful that she would get pregnant, but each month when she found out she was not, she was heartbroken. She had always wanted to be a mother, and every month, she was reminded that she might never be one. This was very difficult for us. It felt as if we were riding a roller coaster of emotions. Each month, hope rose, only to be quashed again and again.

Eventually, we reached the point where our only option was in vitro fertilization. The doctor gave us less than a 1 percent chance without it, but it was stratospherically out of financial reach for a medical student living off student loans. We reached a point where we had become exhausted by the process, emotionally and psychologically. That was when we decided to look into adoption. We began classes with an adoption agency to get approved.

At the beginning of my third year of medical school, our lives changed rapidly. For many years, my wife's younger sister and her husband had been struggling with drug abuse. One day, we arrived at my parent-in-laws' house and found the police were there arresting Teena's brother-in-law for possession.

After this, the state child protective services began investigating them. They decided to flee the state with their toddler daughter to avoid legal trouble. My wife and I tried to convince them by saying, "Just try to stay and work things out. You will make things worse if you leave."

They sharply responded, "We're leaving. If we leave, they can't get us. We're going to the bus to head to another state."

As soon as they left, I called CPS (Child Protective Services) and told them that Teena's sister, Vanessa, and her husband, Ralph, were trying to flee the state. The police met them at the bus stop, arrested them, and took their daughter, Autumn, into custody. The next day, we and Teena's parents had a meeting with the DCFS representative to try to keep Autumn from going into the foster care system.

At two years old, Autumn had lived a difficult life, often blighted by malnutrition and neglect. At this meeting, the social worker went around the room asking my parents-in-law and other family members if any were able to foster the little girl. Eventually, the DCFS representative asked Teena and me if we would be willing to foster Autumn until her birth parents could get their lives back on track. At this point, Teena and I still had not been able to conceive and were on an adoption list.

Both Teena and I responded, "Yes, we will take her."

We were a bit frightened about this opportunity. We agreed Autumn had no other option except the foster care system, and we didn't want that. Autumn was a beautiful, precious soul, and we wanted only the best for her. So we initially agreed to take her in as a foster child, in the hope and belief that her parents could comply with the state services mandate and get their lives together.

The next day, we went to the Ronald McDonald House, where little two-year-old Autumn had been staying. When we saw her, our hearts melted. She was a sad, lonely blonde girl who seemed afraid of her own shadow. She was clinging tightly to a little stuffed, slightly worn teddy bear. She kept this toy for many years and carried it with her all the time.

We hugged her and welcomed her into our family. We became her foster parents for the next six months.

During this time, we also learned that Teena's younger sister was pregnant with another child. This was difficult for my wife as she wondered why her sister, who had lived a life of drugs and chaos, could get pregnant while she could not. She felt that it wasn't fair and wondered why God was punishing us.

Eventually, Teena's sister and her husband came to us and asked, "Do you think it would be best for Autumn if you just adopted her and then adopt our new baby when she is born as well?"

My wife looked at her sister and said, "This is a decision that you have to make and live with for the rest of your life. It's not for us to say."

Her sister went on to say, "We don't feel that we can get where we need to be for Autumn, so . . . would you be willing to adopt her if we give up our rights to her?"

When we first took Autumn, we could not have imagined that we would be adopting her. We thought for sure her parents would do what they needed and get her back. However, without hesitation, thought, or discussion, we replied, "Yes, we will adopt her." We hadn't thought of Autumn as "ours," but what we knew was that, at two years old, this little girl had already experienced more than most of us. She was confused, broken, and scarred. Every time she had to have a visitation with her parents, she would cry for hours afterward, clawing at her skin as if her little soul were trying to escape her tiny body that felt so much confusion and pain. It was more than her mind could comprehend and understand. Even we as adults could not wrap our heads around the situation.

We decided we could easily love and raise Autumn as our own but would do it only with the understanding that she would not have any contact with her birth parents. We felt that she needed time and space to forget everything that had happened to her and start to heal. We proposed this to Teena's sister and her husband, and they agreed.

The next month, we went to court and watched as Autumn's parents relinquished their rights to Autumn. It was a day when sadness and joy strangely clasped hands and became one. I can't begin to verbalize my feelings as I watched her parents give her up. I felt sorry for them and the terrible heartache they were going through. The loss of a child would be theirs to carry through the remainder of their lives, similar to my parents trying to cope with the loss of my brother, Sammy.

However, because of the relinquishment of their parental rights, the process was set into motion for us to adopt Autumn. I also felt joyful at that moment to know we would have a child. We would love her and help her to overcome the hard life that had been hers from birth. The tide for her would change now, and we would be a part of that difference. That day felt akin to a forest fire that nearly devours all life but in doing so allows for a rebirth. When the last ember is put out, the air will clear, and in time a tiny sapling will begin to grow from the ashes to eventually become a full-grown tree sprouting beautiful blossoms. Because of that hope, we felt the joy of imagining Autumn's future and that we would be her parents.

EliAnna

Because unborn children were not recognized by Child Protective Services, the state had no claim to EliAnna (the unborn child we would privately adopt when born) until she was born. Prior to her birth, the assistant attorney general knew of our plans to adopt EliAnna. However, she informed us that in the event the birth parents did not follow through with the adoption to us, we should immediately inform them. The state would then take custody of the child because the parents had never completed the previous requirements to get their other daughter, Autumn, back. They informed us that EliAnna would be considered a sibling at risk. Of course, we never mentioned this to Teena's sister and her husband.

As her sister's pregnancy progressed, Teena began to attend all the prenatal checkups with her. The pregnancy was high risk, and there were concerns about lack of amniotic fluid, lung development, and the baby's small size.

One day my mother asked us, "What are you going to do if she is born disabled or has problems from the mother's drug use?" I thought, *What would you have done if one of your children were born with a disability?* It seemed a ridiculous question to ask someone who was waiting for their baby to be born. And that is what EliAnna was to us, our baby.

It was an exciting, hard, but also crazy time in our lives. It was my third year in medical school, and I was doing clinical rotations in the hospital, often working up to 120 hours per week. I really wasn't home much, but we were excited to be expecting EliAnna to be born and finalizing Autumn's adoption in six months.

Autumn was starting to do better emotionally since she no longer was having visitations with her birth parents. Teena quit working and stayed home with her, something Autumn desperately needed. Every morning, Teena would do Autumn's hair up in pigtails, braids, or curls, put her in front of the mirror, and tell her she was a pretty girl. Teena spent the day taking Autumn to playgroups and the library, and just trying to heal her little broken soul with love. It was a full-time job. I was glad she was able to do it.

Eventually, the time came for EliAnna to be born. Teena was fortunate to be in the room for her birth and see our baby come into this world. After EliAnna was born, Teena stayed in the hospital with her sister and EliAnna, taking care of them the entire time. The adoption papers were drawn up and signed before we took EliAnna home. She weighed only five pounds, and she had the biggest, darkest, most beautiful brown eyes. She was a perfect angel, sent to us from heaven. We buckled her up and brought her home.

As soon as we arrived home, the phone rang. "Teena, this is your sister. We've decided that if you want to keep EliAnna, we want access to Autumn whenever we want."

"I can't do that," replied Teena. "Autumn is our daughter, and she needs to forget everything that has happened so she can heal. I have to do what is right for Autumn."

In a rage, her sister replied, "Then we are f***ing going to come take EliAnna back right now!"

"Sorry, we have to do what's right for Autumn." Teena hung up the phone and looked at me, frantically exclaiming, "What are we going to do?"

Both Teena's sister and her husband had terrible tempers and often became violent. They usually destroyed their apartments by punching holes in the walls or throwing dishes or other objects at each other. We were gravely concerned as now they were headed to our home, and they were raging and out of control. We immediately loaded the girls into the car and started to drive randomly around the city so that we wouldn't be home when they got there.

While we were anxiously driving, we saw a police station. We pulled over and went into the station to explain the situation and ask for help. We used the police station phone to call the attorney general's office to ask for guidance on the best way to proceed. They had told us before EliAnna was born to call them for any situation that might arise.

The police looked up Teena's sister and her husband and saw that they both had outstanding arrest warrants. They said, "We're going to your home and arrest them. We'll lock them up for at least twenty-four hours on these warrants. Hopefully, that will give them some time to cool off and for you guys to figure out what you need to do."

After we waited for several hours at the police station, the representative from the attorney general's office, the guardian ad litem from Child Protective Services (CPS), arrived and took state custody of EliAnna. They then placed her in our care as foster parents. After that, the attorney went to the jail to speak to Teena's sister and her husband. The CPS attorney informed them that EliAnna was now in state custody because of their previous failure to complete the requirements to get Autumn back. We knew they would not take this well and that things were about to get really ugly.

On the Run

Teena and I had twenty-four hours to figure out how we were going to keep ourselves and the girls safe in this very volatile situation. We were afraid of Teena's sister and her husband because of their violent natures and tenuous mental states. We did not know how they would react once they were released from jail and if they were willing to harm us. We decided it was not safe for us to stay at our home, and I knew we could not go to my parents for help. Instead, we drove to my Aunt Jessie and Uncle Phil's home and showed up on their doorstep unannounced. It was getting dark outside, Teena had been crying, and we were exhausted. We explained our situation to them and said, "We have nowhere to go. Can you please help us?"

"Oh my goodness, yes, come in!" My Aunt Jessie took the baby from Teena and told her, "Go take a bath and try to calm yourself. Let me take care of the girls." Aunt Jessie and Uncle Phil made beds up for us, and we stayed with them over the weekend. Our new baby, EliAnna, would sleep only if we held her. I felt that in her little mind she knew she needed us and did not want us to leave her. On Monday morning, I had to go to the hospital for rotations. While I was gone, Teena called and explained our situation to the student housing office. They were very responsive and told us that we could move to any apartment that was vacant. Once I got home, Teena told me that we were moving that night. My uncle, his sons, and I moved us to a new apartment with just a few hours' notice. I will always be grateful to my aunt and uncle for their kindness in helping us in our moment of need.

Let the War Begin

The CPS representative set a court date that Teena's sister and husband would have to attend if they intended to work towards getting EliAnna back. Meanwhile, Teena's sister had gone to a church and told the people that because we were unable to have children, we had taken their children. The deceived church people hired an attorney for Teena's sister and her husband.

The court date came. When we arrived at the courthouse, we saw Teena's sister, her husband, some people from the church, and the attorney they had hired. Their attorney walked up to us and proceeded to badger us with questions.

"Why do you think you can keep those girls? They are not yours," he told us. "That is so shameful of you to take those kids from these wonderful parents. I am going to do everything I can to get them back."

We replied, "We are only foster parents caring for the children. You will have to speak to the guardian ad litem from the attorney general's office. The state has custody of the children."

Shortly after, we were called into the courtroom. When the attorney for CPS presented the case, the incompetent attorney representing the birth parents was blindsided to find out that this wasn't between us and the birth parents but rather between the state of Utah and the birth parents. The more he found out the details of their drug use, warrants, and police records, he stumbled more and more in his speech. Their attorney made quite a fiasco of himself.

However, there was no ambiguity or confusion for the judge or the state's attorneys. The judge informed the parents that they were required to complete the plan made by CPS and the state in order to get EliAnna back. The judge asked if we would be willing to work with them so that the parents could have visitation rights to EliAnna. We told the judge, "We are willing to support the visitations as much as is asked of us."

To protect us from the birth parents, the state asked for us to meet them at a neutral location. They also asked for EliAnna to be picked up by a social worker for her supervised visitations.

At first, the designated people that Teena's sister and husband had chosen would meet us faithfully and on time. It seemed as if they really wanted to have visitations with their daughter. As part of the process, the social worker would also come to our house and tell us how well the birth parents seemed to be doing. She was hopeful that they would be able to get custody back soon. This was a challenging time for us. Mentally and emotionally, we had prepared for EliAnna and in our hearts loved her as our own daughter. The uncertainty about the future of our daughter was one of the hardest things we have endured.

Again and again, the social worker remarked, "The birth parents are doing so well with the CPS plan. It won't be long now before EliAnna can be returned to their custody."

Previously, when we had been foster parents for Autumn, the assistant attorney general told us that Teena's sister and husband had not had a single clean urine drug test, so we asked the social worker, "Have the parents been having clean urine tests, then?"

She responded, "I'm pretty sure. I'll have to check and get back to you." We heard back from her shortly. She informed us that the birth parents had not even been showing up to do their urine drug tests. Additionally, they would not be allowed to have visitations with EliAnna until they'd had multiple negative urine drug tests. This was a relief for us. Calm washed over us. I thought, *Maybe EliAnna will not be taken away from us.*

However, that was just the calm before the storm. Once Teena's sister and husband found out that they actually had to start showing up for the drug tests, they became really nasty. They began to use even more deception. Teena's sister would call and cancel visitations with us, then immediately call the social worker to state that we were refusing to allow the visitations. They were attempting to get EliAnna removed from our care and moved into a foster home. We began to document these calls. It was a nightmare.

EliAnna had been unsettled from the moment she was born. We always assumed it was because she had been born with drugs in her system and was probably going through withdrawal. She would have to be held all night to get her to sleep. Because of the strife created by her birth parents, we felt despondent. Teena would sit up with the baby at night, feed her, and cry. "I don't think I can do this anymore," she said. "They could come and take her away any day, and I can't bear it."

"You have to bear it for EliAnna, Teena. You have to," I told her.

"I feel like I'm on the verge of a mental breakdown," said my sweet wife.

"Honey, you can do this," I encouraged her.

Shortly after, Teena's sister and husband stopped the visitations altogether, and EliAnna got sick with RSV (respiratory syncytial virus). She became quite ill and was hospitalized. When they admitted her, we explained the custody situation to the hospital staff, including the birth parents' violent past and criminal records. We asked if there was a way to ensure that Teena's sister and husband would not be able to gain access to EliAnna in the hospital without going through their social worker. We were concerned that they would lie to the hospital staff and tell them that she was their daughter and take her home. The hospital staff was very responsive and placed the hospital floor on lockdown so no unauthorized person could gain access.

The next day, we heard that Teena's sister and husband had broken into a home and stolen baby items and a car and were now wanted by the law. Our hearts sank at the thought they had surely planned to try to take EliAnna from the hospital and flee the state. We felt gratitude for the caring hospital staff who had protected her. After this, Teena would not leave the hospital until EliAnna came home.

No one had any idea where the parents had gone. Their home had been completely trashed with garbage and personal items scattered all over the floor. They had punched several holes in the walls. It looked as if they had fled in a hurry. This left us feeling afraid and on the edge for some time, not knowing where they were or what they were planning.

The attorney general's office told us that they would post a summons in all the surrounding areas so that if the parents did not show up for a court hearing, their parental rights would be terminated. The day came, and we found ourselves back in court. The court terminated the birth parents' parental rights to EliAnna. During the hearing, the judge looked sternly at us and said, "You are not to allow the birth parents any visitation with EliAnna of any type." We wholeheartedly agreed.

We then began the process to adopt EliAnna. We would have to wait six months before we could finalize the adoption, and then EliAnna would forever be ours. Meanwhile, the longer Teena's sister and her husband were missing, the more we felt at ease. However, we knew that most kidnapped children are taken by people they know, and this would be a worry that we would carry over the next decade.

In this short span of time in my third year of medical school, we had become foster parents to a toddler and a newborn, in addition to raising my wife's teenage sister. It was an overwhelming, dramatic change.

At this point, we were able to proceed with the adoption of both Autumn and EliAnna. We loved them dearly and wanted them to be our daughters and part of our family. The day of the adoption came. We stood in front of the judge as he finalized the adoptions. We were very grateful to an attorney friend who had carried out the adoption pro bono for us.

THE THIRD-YEAR BLUR

It was during the third year of medical school when this whole adoption episode transpired, the year hospital rotations and clinics began. This time in medical school is when you start to live medicine and become a clinical physician. It is the most demanding year of medical school, when you often spend 100 to 120-plus hours per week in the hospital.

Because of everything that was happening, most of that third year of medical school is actually a blur to me. I remember spending time with my daughters and my wife at home or on some holidays, but other than that, I really lack many other memories of that time outside of the hospital.

After we were blessed with our two daughters, I wanted to spend more time with them, which was difficult due to the demands of school, both the time spent at the hospital and the amount of studying. I felt inadequate as a father as I was not able to spend as much time as I wanted with my children. Thus, to spend time with them and study, I came up with the idea of reading to them from my textbooks at bedtime instead of normal bedtime stories. I thought it was a good compromise. For example, I would read from my medical physiology text and use a fun kid's voice that made it seem as if it were a children's book. They seemed to enjoy it, and they liked looking at some of the physiology diagrams. It was a good way for me to spend time with them and keep up with my studies. Sometimes I would lie down on the floor next to the girls to just be by them while I rested my eyes. More than once I would wake up with little barrettes or ribbons in my hair that Autumn had clipped in while I slept.

EliAnna's developing personality was anything but little. She was like a constant beam of sunshine. She always had a smile on her face. Most babies fuss when their clothes are changed, but not EliAnna. EliAnna would look up at us with those huge brown eyes and beautiful smile. We would pull her clothes either off her or on her, and as soon as they moved past her eyes, she looked at us and smiled as if we were playing "hide 'n' peek." She still couldn't sleep well, and we would later learn that she never would, but she just brought us so much joy. Teena would call her "Sunshine," and sunshine she was. You never saw a happier baby.

During this third year of medical school, the hospital didn't have any limits on hours worked during rotations, so many times I would end up at the hospital for twenty-four, thirty, or forty-plus hours straight. Some weeks I spent more than 115 hours a week at the hospital. In addition to learning to take care of patients, I also had to learn the textbook material. When I had downtime, I had to study the principles of internal medicine or surgery or other subjects. I would still attend church at the hospital when I was able to, as they would have church services on Sundays for the patients and residents.

During this year, I intentionally chose the most rigorous rotation schedule I could to challenge myself to be the best I could be. I approached each rotation as if I would be doing that for my entire life. I had used this approach my entire life. For example, when I was young, when I worked as a cook, I worked as hard as if it were going to be my job for the rest of my life.

I carried this work ethic into my medical training. For example, when I did surgery, I approached it as if I were going to be a surgeon. When I did internal medicine, I worked as if I were going to be an internist. I did each rotation with the same goal of putting 110 percent of my effort into it. My philosophy was that I might not always be the smartest or the most charismatic person in the room, but I could always choose to be the hardest working.

PLASTIC SURGERY ROTATION

I remember vividly that plastic surgery was my first rotation. It was surreal to be literally one day in the classroom and the next day in the operating room, scrubbing in to help on a case. I remember my first time was quite intimidating. I spent quite some time scrubbing in to make sure I washed my hands properly. Then the scrub nurse checked me over. This was followed by learning how to gown up and glove up correctly. The first time I was awkward, fumbled around, dropped my glove on the ground, and touched something nonsterile, contaminating myself. The nurse promptly sent me back outside to start over and scrub my hands again. I felt as if I were back in kindergarten learning how to jump rope again. After this, I became much better in the OR and had many wonderful experiences there.

One of my most challenging rotations was surgery. Every Thursday, we had a very long case that lasted anywhere from ten to twelve hours. During that time, you couldn't leave the operating room unless you had an emergency. Even leaving the operation to eat or drink, go to the bathroom, or pretty much do anything besides help with the case was seen as a sign of weakness. In preparation for that day, the night before I would not drink much water to intentionally dehydrate myself so that the next day, I would not have to go to the bathroom.

A funny thing happened to me during this rotation. One day, I found myself famished and had not eaten for quite some time. I went into the lounge, and there was a large platter of a variety of donuts sitting there. Some of these were cream filled, and I happened to grab one because I was starving. It tasted pretty good, but it was a decision I would come to regret. Later that night, I had terrible cramping abdominal pain and explosive diarrhea. I ended up with food poisoning from the cream in the donut because it had sat out too long.

I was so sick that night with profuse vomiting and severe diarrhea that I could not even stand up. I am sure I had a terrible fever and became dehydrated. I was so sick and nauseated that I literally lay on the cold ceramic tile bathroom floor by the toilet because I couldn't move. A reasonable person would have stayed home the next morning rather than go into the hospital. However, medical students are not always the most reasonable with their own health, so what did I do?

The next morning, I got up and went back to the hospital to continue my surgery rotation. It was a bit difficult, though, standing through ordinary cases with my abdominal cramping and feeling that I was going to have diarrhea for several hours.

THE GOOD, THE BAD, THE BIZARRE

Most of the attending physicians, as the supervising doctors were known in medical school, were just awesome to work with. Dr. Brant was one of them. He invited students to work with him and regularly found projects for us to do. He was a very kind, passionate, and knowledgeable professional. He approached everything with a cheerful, unflappable demeanor and was respectful to nurses, staff, and medical students alike.

After my tenure working with him extensively on several projects, I received a very nice letter of recommendation, which helped secure my residency at Johns Hopkins. The vast majority of the attendings at medical school were like that—obliging, insightful, and supportive.

Contrast that with Dr. M. Dr. M. was notorious in his treatment of residents, nursing staff, and medical students, so I was chagrined to find out that I was assigned to his surgical team. As soon as I arrived for the rotation, the surgical resident quickly explained what the expectations were "Speak when spoken to, do not speak otherwise, and be prepared to answer any question he may ask, no matter how long you have been standing there. You go to your assigned place in the operating room, and you do not move, shuffle, or do anything distracting for the entire length of the surgical procedure, no matter its duration, even for many hours. You also arrive early before he does, see patients beforehand on your own, and write notes. After that, you attend the surgical rounds with the surgical team—and that's *before* launching into the day's surgery."

Each day, I dutifully arrived at the hospital at 4:00 a.m., an hour and a half before everyone else on the team, to do my rounds. The first day in the OR, the resident motioned to me where I was to stand near the patient. I stood in that place for the next hour and a half without speaking and tried to pay attention.

Eventually, however, my focus started to fade, and my mind began to wander as I thought about what I could be doing for fun out in the sunshine. Suddenly, Dr. M. abruptly asked me, "Student [he did not bother to learn medical students' names], what am I doing in this part of the procedure?"

I quickly snapped my attention back to the present, panic-stricken. The surgical resident quickly recognized my predicament and kindly gave me a little clue to aid my answer. Thankfully, I had read beforehand about this particular procedure and, with the clue, answered Dr. M.'s question to his satisfaction. He did not speak to me for the rest of the procedure, which took an hour longer.

A little later in the OR, I discovered firsthand why Dr. M. had such a notorious reputation. When the scrub nurse handed him an instrument that he didn't like, he proceeded to yell at her, spewing profanities. He then threw the instrument back on the tray and asked for another one. The nurse handed him a second instrument that he also took exception to, and he promptly threw it back on the tray, using such foul language that it took my breath away. The nurse apologized and tried a third instrument, and this one he threw across the room. He finally received an instrument that he liked, but I stood there aghast at this kind of behavior. He reminded me of a toddler throwing a tantrum.

After the procedure, the resident told me, "Yeah, that's a common occurrence with him." He advised, "It's just best to keep your head down, get through the few weeks of the rotation, and avoid the wrath of Dr. M." I wisely followed his sage advice. Consequently, I spent those few weeks flying under the radar and looking forward to emerging into the civilized company of my other colleagues.

Then there was Dr. W., an attending I worked with later in my training. He was just bizarre. He was a Vietnam veteran who had served with the Green Berets. Everybody who had known him before he'd left for Vietnam claimed that he was not the same when he came back. There were many rumors floating around about him in the hospital, such as that he had assaulted another physician, that he carried a knife with him, that he threatened people, and that he had performed an autopsy on his father. Of course, I thought those were just rumors.

But one day, when another of my colleagues and I were working with Dr. W., he started explaining the significance of mitral annulus calcifications, and then midsentence stated nonchalantly, "When I was assisting on the autopsy of my father, this is what we found."

My jaw hit the floor, and I gasped. I was totally speechless. *The rumor was true?!* I didn't know how to respond to that . . . performing a medical autopsy on a parent. That idea was considered bizarre even by medical standards.

Later on, Dr. W. told us how to approach a case as if we were going to stab it: "You don't stab from above because they can block that. You go from below, right for the heart of the case." I appreciated the metaphor, even though it was a bit macabre.

He would also give us just five to ten seconds to answer his questions. At other times, he would quip with wise words such as "If you want to kill the patient, why don't you just push them down the stairs? It would be faster."

On another occasion, he looked over at my colleague Mike and said, "Mike, come to the basement with me." Mike glanced around with a slightly panicked look that said, *Is he going to chop me into little bits?* I returned his look with a shrug that meant, *I have no idea.*

Mike went down to the hospital basement with Dr. W. There, Dr. W. pointed to a chin-up bar he had set up and said, "Mike, let's see how many pull-ups you can do."

Mike was baffled but relieved as he had thought he was going to be murdered in the basement, with his body left for his distraught colleagues to find. Mike did as many pull-ups as he could, and Dr. W. was satisfied.

Dr. W. had many other unusual quirks. As with Dr. M., I spent my time with him keeping my head down, avoiding his wrath by flying under the radar, and looking forward to moving on from this eccentric character.

At the end of third year, I found out that I was being inducted into the Alpha Omega Alpha Honor Society, which is for the top 10 to 15 percent of the graduating class. It was quite a prestigious honor. I had also done well on the first part of the licensing board test. That first board score is important to determine your residency program selection. Residency is the required three-to-seven-year training program that medical school graduates must complete before they can become doctors working without supervision. It is also when a doctor becomes trained in a specialty. If you don't do well on that first board exam, you won't be able to apply to certain residency programs.

CHAPTER 28

Residency Applications

At the beginning of my fourth year of medical school, I applied for residency. I made sure to apply to a wide range of programs—I think fifteen—to make sure I would get into at least one. I was not sure I would match because of my inner dialogue about being afraid to fail, a result of my life growing up. One of the top-rated residency programs was at Johns Hopkins. I told myself, *Why not apply there? The worst that can happen is they will say no. If I get rejected, that's okay, and I'll move forward.* It was a shooting star dream that I would even get a chance to interview there, much less get accepted.

My wife and I were still poor, which made it difficult to afford going to interviews. We were now raising our two adopted children and Teena's youngest sister, who was thirteen going on fourteen at this time. In order to save money, I tried to arrange my interviews geographically so I could fly to one and then drive to several others without having to fly again.

Back then, we had to navigate using a map or MapQuest-printed directions. One time, I flew to Iowa in the winter, in mid-December. There was a huge snowstorm, and I had to drive across Iowa to Omaha, Nebraska for an interview. Using my MapQuest-printed directions and my map book, I had to drive all the way across the state in one day as my interview was the next morning. The conditions became so severe with the blizzard, there were complete whiteout conditions. I could see only maybe ten to fifteen feet in front of me at most, and I was praying the whole time that I would not veer off the road and freeze to death in some snowbank. I honestly don't like to think back on it because it was pretty much white-knuckle driving for several hours. I did not have a cell phone at the time, so the risk was real.

As I was driving, a semi-truck passed me on the road, splashing snow and ice all over my windshield, temporarily blinding me. "Oh no! I can't see!" I exclaimed loudly. "Now it's even worse! I'm going to slide off the road, and they won't find my frozen body for hours!"

I began to panic. My palms started to sweat, and my heart rate skyrocketed. I took a deep breath, paused, and turned on the windshield wipers. I then saw that the semi-truck was actually a blessing as I was able to now follow it down the road because it contrasted nicely against the snow, and I could drive in the tracks it made. Miraculously, I made it to Omaha and had my interview the next day. Immediately after it, I had to catch a flight from there to another interview. I quickly drove to the airport, and I literally made the last flight of the day because all those after it were canceled due to the weather.

I interviewed at Mayo Clinic, which I really enjoyed. Then I was shocked to get an interview invitation to Johns Hopkins in Baltimore. There, I was interviewed by several residents and faculty and also by Dr. Siegelman, the residency program director. He was a legend in the radiology field, as he had been the editor of *Radiology*, the premier medical journal in what would become my field, for several decades and had been the program director at Hopkins for around thirty years. He had also trained more radiology department chairs and program directors than anyone in the country.

I was quite intimidated to be interviewed by him. He asked me several questions, including a little about my history as a homeless teenager (I had included a brief statement about being homeless in my application). Most applicants came from Ivy League schools with fairly well-off parents. I was not in either of those camps. Dr. Siegelman had never met someone with my background who had completed medicine, let alone at the top of their class. It made me stand out. Dr. Siegelman was looking for more than just a good resident, he wanted a well-rounded resident. That I had overcome homelessness to graduate from medical school helped him see me as an exceptional candidate. I found it intriguing that what I once considered one of my life's greatest weaknesses was now becoming a strength.

The interview took place in a large office, with the distinguished gray-haired Dr. Siegelman wearing a yellow-brown sport coat and a white shirt and tie. He had that intimidating professor look, but he was quite gracious and kind. I remember I felt overwhelmed even to be interviewing at a place like Johns Hopkins. He ultimately became one of my favorite attending physicians and someone I truly admire.

I also was able to tour the lab of Elliot Fishman. Before my Johns Hopkins interview, I had looked up people in the department to find out what they were researching. I was so excited to be able to tour the 3D lab as I had found out quite a bit about it. Elliott Fishman is one of the pioneers in 3D medical imaging. When I saw what he was doing, I was enamored by it, and I loved how cutting edge it was. As I toured the lab, I thought, *Wow, it would be really cool one day to work in this lab.*

When I got home, I told Teena that Hopkins was one of my top choices but still really did not think there was a chance I would be able to get in because they normally had over seven hundred applicants for six positions. Doing the math, that was less than a 1 percent chance.

I went home and hoped for the best.

CHAPTER 29

Match Day

atch Day is a unique experience when all medical students find out where they have been matched for residency and whether they will be training in the specialty of their choice. Most people bring someone with them with whom to share the moment. Some people bring their spouses or significant others; one person even brought their mother. I chose the most important person in my life, Teena, my wife, to attend.

For the event, we dressed up nicely. I put on a shirt and tie, and Teena put on a nice dress. We met in an auditorium at the university. They had round tables set up all across the room with centerpieces to highlight each medical school class. The medical school also set up a small buffet table for snacks and hors d'oeuvres.

Teena and I found a table in the corner and sat down. The MC announced how the process was going to work. Each medical student would stand up and walk to the table that had all the names laid out with envelopes. In the envelope was a letter that stated where they had been matched for their residency location and where they would spend the next three to seven years of their lives.

I looked around the room at the faces I had spent so much time with for the past four years. I thought about some of the events that had transpired. We had learned together, laughed together, and cried together over our murdered classmate, and we all had worked very hard to earn those initials behind our names: MD. We literally had shared blood, sweat, and tears. I will always remember my classmates and treasure the times I spent with them.

We followed alphabetical order, so I was toward the end of the program. I listened with excitement as each of my fellow students announced where they would train for their residency. The anticipation and excitement crescendoed in me.

When it was my turn, I walked over and retrieved my envelope. I tore it open. My jaw almost hit the floor when I read, "The Johns Hopkins Hospital and School of Medicine, Baltimore, Maryland."

I was shocked, delightfully surprised, and beyond happy to see those words. It was my top choice, a prestigious school, and deep down, I think I had convinced myself that my dicey background was going to prevent me from ever being accepted there.

When I shared the results of my match with my classmates, I felt like I was walking on a cloud. I said, "Johns Hopkins," and my classmates applauded. I said my thanks to my classmates, said what a wonderful group of folks they were, and thanked them for being my friends. I went back to the table and hugged and kissed my wife.

Shortly after the event, when we were mingling, a classmate of mine who had always tried to compete with me came up to me. I think she missed where I had said I was going, and she had come over to "humble brag" about herself. She proudly told me where she had matched. It was somewhere in the Midwest; I don't even remember where. I told her that I had matched at the Johns Hopkins University School of Medicine.

She had a stunned look on her face, was speechless for a moment, and then asked, "Are you okay with that?"

I started laughing. I said, "Of course I'm okay with that. It is one of the top institutions in the world. Why wouldn't I be okay with that?"

I think she was just trying to save face.

I was finishing my fourth year of medical school by doing a rotation in family practice at a rural site in southern Utah several hours away from the main campus. I did this to learn more about rural medicine and so Teena and I could get away to a warmer place for a while. One day, Teena picked me up from the clinic, and she just looked radiant and glowing. She had a huge smile on her face.

I looked at her and thought, *What is going on?*

She excitedly exclaimed, "I'm pregnant!"

We felt it was a miracle as we had given up all hope of ever having biological children.

CHAPTER 30

Moving On

GRADUATION

Eventually, after innumerable hours, sleepless nights, and endless studying, medical school came to an end. Graduation day was here! I invited my parents to commencement, not sure if they would come. The ceremony was held at Kingsbury Hall, the same building where they did the white coat ceremony four years earlier, though it seemed as if an eternity had passed.

I dressed in my doctoral robes with the stripes on the sleeves, eager for the time I could officially call myself "Doctor." I, of course, brought the most important people in my life—my wife and children—to the ceremony.

When I arrived, I saw that most of my classmates, dressed in their graduation robes with their own important people, had already arrived. I found my seat in the auditorium and looked around. In the mezzanine, I spotted my parents. Mom had her usual angry look, as if she were mad at someone or something, probably Dad.

The ceremony was convened. I sat patiently listening to the names of my fellow classmates as each was called and each person was subsequently "hooded" with the doctoral hood. Finally, my name was called: "Christopher L. Smith."

This time was different from four years ago. Now, I knew I could do it, that I could do difficult things. I had completed what Mom thought I could never do. I was not a "screwup," as she had told me. I had achieved the first step of my dreams. I glanced at my wife, gave her a crooked smile, as if to say, *Thank you for supporting me and taking this journey with me.*

I arose and walked up to the stage to receive my diploma and doctoral hood. As I walked, a variety of thoughts passed through my head. I was grateful for this incredible opportunity I had been given, the privilege of being a physician and taking care of people. I also knew that I had not accomplished this myself. I recognized many people who had helped me along the path. Internally, I thanked all those people. I also thanked my wife as I know that I could not have accomplished these goals without her support. Most importantly, I recognized the hand of God, who had lifted me and carried me along to reach this point.

I reached the stage and slowly leaned forward as the dean placed the hood over my head. Inside, I exploded with joy and happiness, ecstatic to have reached this point. I walked over and picked up my diploma, which was in a cardboard tube to protect it. As soon as I returned to my seat, I opened the tube and stared at the diploma.

It said, "The School of Medicine has conferred upon Christopher Leon Smith the degree of Doctor of Medicine, with all its Rights, Honors, and Responsibilities."

A part of me couldn't believe seeing my name with "Doctor of Medicine." It was a surreal moment. I had actually done it!

It seemed so long ago that I was doing dishes at the restaurant and dreaming of bigger things, such as being a shift manager at the restaurant. Yet here I was now, a Doctor of Medicine. It seemed so far out of the stratosphere for me, yet, through hard work, some talent, grit, and stoic stubbornness to continue striving despite failing, I had made it through one of the most rigorous education processes one can, medical school.

After the ceremony, we stood around taking pictures. My parents walked up to me, and Dad gave me a hug, saying, "I am proud of you, son."

Mom just said, "Wow, I can't believe you actually did it."

Mom, also seemingly wanting to take away from the moment or put the spotlight on her, invited me to a "celebration party" at their house. Based on my prior experiences with her "hosting parties" and wheelbarrow race, I declined and said I had other plans.

I did what I wanted to, spending time with those who truly believed in and cared for me. I went to a graduation dinner with my wife and children.

I knew at this point that I did not need my mother's approval or support. I had others who would lift me. I had found my own circle of love outside of my parents. I had also realized that I would likely never receive a seal of approval from my mother. In her eyes, I might always be a "screwup," but I didn't care anymore. I had moved on, breaking her control over me, and I knew that I was now a doctor of medicine and that no matter what my mother said, she could never take that away from me!

LEAVING UTAH

The four years of medical school had passed, sometimes quickly, other times at a snail's pace. Our family had grown to two children, plus Ange and one more on the way. We had been blessed in many ways. The next task for us was to move our growing family over two thousand miles to do a required one-year internship in Roanoke, Virginia, prior to starting residency at Johns Hopkins (radiology requires a one-year general internship—with rotations in surgery, internal medicine, emergency medicine, OB/GYN, and pediatrics—before starting a diagnostic radiology residency).

Teena and I loaded all our belongings into a ten-by-ten-foot space on a trailer that would be shipped to our new apartment in Virginia. Our next task was to get our Honda minivan and children across the country.

Teena and I ultimately decided that we would drive across the country with our van, then fly back and pick up our kids. We had left them with Teena's parents while we drove to Virginia as we thought they might be too young to handle a trip like that.

We departed Utah in mid-June, leaving the nice sunny weather. We headed towards Wyoming and the high mountain passes towards Cheyenne. Suddenly, as we drove across the pass in Wyoming, a blizzard with near-whiteout conditions hit us. I looked at Teena and said, "Well, all we can do is keep going. There isn't anything else around."

We slowed to a crawl as the snow continued to fly all around us. Finally, after several hours, we made it down the valley and reached Cheyenne, the last city before the plains. The blizzard had put us a few hours behind. Our goal was to drive straight across to Virginia without stopping, taking turns driving.

We headed out across Nebraska. Nebraska is flat with cornfields as far as the eye can see. When driving, the scene never seems to change. It feels like hours and hours of cornfields. We drove for many hours, and night set in. I looked over at Teena, who was five months pregnant, and she looked exhausted. So rather than ask her to spell me, I just kept driving.

Around midnight, I was starting to feel like I was in a haze. I asked Teena, "Do you want to stop somewhere?"

She quickly responded, "Yes. I don't think I can stand much more driving."

I felt bad for her as, being pregnant, she had to be uncomfortable sitting that long. However, she was amazing and never complained once. I looked around. We were in the middle of nowhere in the plains, somewhere in Nebraska with no hotels in sight. I told Teena, "I don't see anywhere to stop, and plus, I don't think we can afford much of a hotel room." We needed all our money to get us the rest of the way to Virginia and to pay a deposit on the new apartment.

A few miles down the road, I saw an exit to a small farm off the freeway and asked Teena, "We can pull over there and sleep if you want?"

She agreed wholeheartedly.

I pulled off the exit, onto the side of the road, and turned the car off. We made a bed the best we could for Teena in the back fold-down seat, and I lay down to rest as well. I ended up getting a few hours of restless sleep. I could never fall into a deep sleep as I was worried about Teena and wanted to make sure no one tried to break into the car.

Finally, the sun came up, and we decided to start driving again. Another long day passed with many hours of driving and another restless night at a rest stop. The drive stretched on forever, with occasional bathroom and McDonald's food stops.

Eventually, we saw the sign that said, "Welcome to Roanoke, Star City of the South." Roanoke has a large star on a hill for which it is known. I felt huge relief as we had finally arrived. The truck with our belongings was set to arrive the next day. We decided to splurge and stay at a motel that night to get some rest. I also picked up dinner at that iconic southern restaurant Waffle House.

The next day, the truck with our trailer arrived, and we had twenty-four hours to unload it. Teena stayed in the house unpacking rather than doing heavy lifting so she didn't risk her pregnancy. I started to unload the truck; however, one thing I didn't count on was the extreme heat and humidity of the South in late June. Utah is a dry, arid state. Virginia felt like a swamp with such stifling heat, I could taste it. For many hours, I struggled to unload the truck by myself, drenched in large pools of sweat.

As I was about to give up for the day, our neighbor's teenage son came out and asked, "Do you need some help?"

I almost hugged him for his hospitality! I quickly responded in the affirmative, and he jumped in to help. The work went much, much faster with him helping, and we emptied the rest of the truck.

When we finished, I offered to pay him. He kindly responded in his nice Virginia accent, "No sir. In the South, we are happy to help our neighbors. I couldn't take your money. It wouldn't be right. No sir, my ma would be disappointed in me. I just wanted to help y'all out."

I was humbled by his kindness and offered to feed him and his mom (a single parent) dinner when we got settled in. He said, "Sure, I would love to come over for some grits. See you then," and he left.

I have never forgotten our young neighbor's kindness in helping me and his unselfish attitude. I think he is an example for all of us to follow: to do good in the world without expectation of reward. If more people were like that, the world would be a much kinder, gentler place.

CHAPTER 31

Haley

At the end of her pregnancy with our daughter, whom we named Haley, while I was in my internship year in Virginia before starting at Hopkins, Teena began to have complications. That last month before she was supposed to deliver, I was on my emergency medicine rotation, where I did three nights and then three days on with one day off. It alternated every week and was quite tiresome. One night when I was on my emergency medicine rotation, I arrived home to find Teena doubled over in pain on the couch. She was breathing heavily, doing Lamaze-type breathing. We were worried she might have been going into early labor, four to five weeks prior to her expected delivery.

She asked me to take her to the hospital, and I agreed. The doctors found she was having contractions, but they were caused by a kidney stone. They gave her medicine through her IV to help stop the pain and contractions. We were able to return home later that night and hoped for the best.

I came home another day to find Teena again having severe pain and contractions. We went to the hospital, and they decided to admit her this time. They found that she was having more kidney stones, causing her to go into labor. Her pain was immense and she was in her last trimester, so they ended up keeping her for about a week.

While she was in the hospital, I was on my own to take care of our two young children and Teena's twelve-year-old sister. I was still on my emergency medicine three-day/three-night rotation. In residency, it is very difficult to change shifts or get additional time off, so I bit the bullet and continued to work. I worked overnight in the emergency room while my neighbor watched my children. I then came home, took care of my children, slept for maybe two or three hours, and then went back to the hospital. I did this for that entire week. I was so exhausted by the time it was over, I felt as if I would fall asleep standing up.

At the end of the week, they decided to induce labor to relieve the pressure on Teena's kidneys. They started the Pitocin infusion, and Teena's pain increased significantly as she had labor pains compounded by kidney pain. They attempted to do an epidural, but she still did not get adequate pain relief.

At this point, Teena was losing quite a bit of blood because of stones in her kidneys and was shaking uncontrollably from the labor combined with renal (kidney) pain. Dr. Gardner, the ob-gyn, looked at me and said, "We are going to have to do an emergency C-section."

We all gowned up, and Teena was rolled to the OR. I sat next to her head by the anesthesiologist and held her hand. I watched her eyes and prayed that she would be okay. She looked at me and said she was excited to see our baby girl. Dr. Gardner began to make the cesarean incision.

When the obstetricians delivered Haley, they held her up above the table to show her to us. They then took her to another table to dry her off and clean her.

The nurse asked me, "Do you want to come meet your daughter?"

I said, "Yes, I would like that very much."

I looked into my daughter's beautiful brown eyes for the first time and felt she was the most amazing thing I had ever seen. I thought she was perfect in every way.

However, as soon as I welcomed her to the world, the charge nurse came over to speak to me. She said, "Dr. Smith, you have to leave immediately. Your wife is in serious trouble and is having complications. You need to leave so we can resuscitate her and take care of her."

I was shocked and didn't know what to say as just a few moments before, everything had been going well. I glanced over at Teena and saw frenzied activity as they were rapidly putting a breathing tube down her throat and beginning resuscitation. I saw that Teena was completely unresponsive and ashen. Vivid memories of my baby brother as they pulled him from the water rapidly flashed in my eyes. I was worried her heart had stopped and she was dying.

One of the other nurses ushered me out to the waiting room near the OR. It was an older waiting room with hard plastic pastel-colored chairs and a cold vinyl ugly green-colored floor. It was also completely empty as it was around one o'clock in the morning. The nurse quickly explained that she had to go back to help revive my wife and promptly left, leaving me completely alone, shocked at the sudden change in events, expecting the other shoe to drop on my wonderful life that was just beginning to blossom. The nurse did not give me any further details about what had transpired or if my wife still lived.

As I sat alone and uncomfortable in the cold waiting room, my thoughts began to spiral out of control. The memory of the long, slow ride in the hearse with the cold dead body of my brother flashed in my mind. I shivered slightly, whether due to the memory, the chill of the waiting room, or a combination of both I'm not sure.

My thoughts ran amok like a cyclone in my mind. I imagined myself in another long, slow hearse ride, this time with the love of my life, my wife's cold corpse accompanying me. I couldn't bear the thought of that possibility; it tore at my soul. I was devastated, fractured, and terrified of being alone again.

Alone.

Alone.

The word pounded loudly in my thoughts, echoing again and again, reverberating in my mind. The emotional pain swelled within me, memories of my little brother combined with the possible loss of Teena. I couldn't breathe. My heart pounded in my chest as I felt the room spinning, closing in on me. I thought of my beautiful daughter Haley and imagined having to someday tell her that her mother died giving birth to her. I didn't have a backup plan as I normally did. I didn't have anything. I was at a loss, crushed and broken.

Fear consumed me; loneliness overwhelmed me. I couldn't imagine raising my daughters by myself. I felt empty, my soul beginning to fracture because Teena was my light, my life, and she completed me. I didn't have anyone to turn to, to hold me, to comfort me. *I was completely alone in this dark empty place.*

Tears welled in my eyes, and I looked up to heaven. At that moment, I did the only thing I could. I knelt down on the cold, hard floor of the waiting room, and I prayed. I prayed as I had never prayed, with an urgency driven by the total devastation of my soul that ravaged me.

I pleaded with God, "Please let her live. I can't survive without her. She is my life, my everything, and without her, I am worried the darkness will consume me."

I continued pleading, kneeling on that cold, unforgiving floor, pouring my soul out to God. I implored, "God, I would be willing to give my life in exchange for hers, but I know it doesn't work that way. Please hear me, and if it be thy will, let her stay with us."

Eventually, I ran out of energy and words. I stayed there kneeling on the floor, completely exhausted from lack of sleep and the emotional pain of it all, but I was consumed by fear, unable to rest, to feel peace or calm while Teena remained in the operating room.

Fear: Sometimes it is as palpable as a dense fog, smothering even the air we breathe. It permeates every corner of the mind. Fear is born from distrusting oneself or others. Fear feeds on anxiety over the unknown. To not let that fear overwhelm and crush your soul, you have to trust: trust yourself, trust others, and trust God. Then you can move forward and not lose sight of the goal despite being afraid. The fear will still be there, but it will be overshadowed by love and trust. Ultimately, as love and trust drive away the fear, even though you may be broken, scarred, and afraid, your soul will truly live and love, able to experience the joy that life can bring.

I finally mustered the strength to move on. I picked myself up from the floor and sat down again. I stared pensively at the clock, its soft ticking echoing in the empty room. I waited and waited for any news, good or bad.

I sat on those hard, uncomfortable plastic chairs expecting the worst, wondering if the love of my life was going to die, with only the deafening silence and the constant ticking of the clock to comfort or entertain me.

After a couple of hours of this solitary prison of silence, Teena still was not out of the OR. The nursery nurse came down and asked me, "Do you want to give your baby her first bottle? She's hungry."

I quickly agreed, wanting anything to distract me from my terrible imaginings. I promptly followed the nurse to the nursery and found our new daughter, Haley.

As soon as I held her, I looked at her beautiful eyes and talked to her, telling her she was a beautiful little girl and how perfect she was. I did not know if my wife was still alive or had passed away, so I sat there alone in the nursery, clinging to our baby and dreading the worst.

I received some comfort in the idea that at least I would always have a small part of Teena in our daughter Haley. I let my thoughts wander for some time, cradling this precious daughter of mine, not wanting to let her go. Eventually, I made my way back down to the waiting room, again to wait alone in silence and listen to the ticking clock echoing in the room, all the while imagining the worst-case scenario.

Finally, after several hours, the quiet, lonely hell in which I was trapped ended. The same nurse had arrived to update me.

She told me, "Teena is out of the operating room and is in the recovery room. As soon as they delivered the baby, Teena stopped breathing. They had to put her on a ventilator to keep her alive. Thankfully the anesthesiologist was right there with her and was able to do that quickly. We're having a hard time waking her up and getting her to respond. Maybe having you there will help her. Do you want to come back?"

Joy and relief washed over me, and I knew that God had heard me and answered my prayer. Teena's eyes were still closed as I stepped next to her bedside. I grabbed her hand and beckoned her to open her eyes. She finally fluttered her eyes open and looked at me. They had just pulled her breathing tube before I came back, so she struggled to speak. The nurse kept checking her abdomen, became concerned, left, and came back with the doctor.

The doctor said, "We need to take her back to the OR. It appears that she has internal bleeding that is expanding and hemorrhaging into her abdomen."

Teena looked at me with frantic eyes and just kept struggling to mutter, "No, no, no."

I looked at her and said, "You have to go. It will be alright." I looked to the nurse and said, "Go ahead and take her. She just doesn't understand."

Teena's tear-filled eyes looked to me in desperation with her struggling "no"s. I watched as her hand left mine, and they took her again. I found myself again in the cold waiting room on the hard plastic chairs, waiting for another couple of hours while they worked on controlling Teena's bleeding.

Eventually, they finished and told me I could go see Teena. She was doing okay but would be in the hospital for several days. Once Teena was able to rest and the anesthesia wore off, she told me that she had been aware the whole time while they resuscitated her and could hear everything that was going on. She couldn't move, talk, or see but was aware of everything else. It was a living nightmare, feeling completely powerless, losing the ability to breathe, paralyzed, and essentially trapped in a black box. She thought she had been in a coma during that time, that she would never make it back. She would go on to relive the memory in her nightmares for many months to come.

I called my mother-in-law and updated her, desperately asking for her help because I knew I couldn't keep working without sleeping for much longer, especially with the baby. My mother-in-law agreed to come and help us take care of the baby. I then called my residency and told them the situation. I had to use one of my three weeks of vacation to take care of my family.

CHAPTER 32

Hopkins

I finished the rest of that year, and my first days at Johns Hopkins arrived. I was a fresh-faced youngster having completed the one-year internship in Virginia. We residents had a modest welcome luncheon, and then the department chair invited us into his office so we could meet him and each other.

His office was quite large and had a conference room adjacent to it. He took us back into the conference room, where a large table had about ten chairs arranged around it. We sat down and began to introduce ourselves to each other and briefly share something about ourselves. One of my fellow residents had just arrived overnight from Germany and his luggage had been delayed, so he showed up in Levi's and a button-down shirt. The rest of us were dressed up in shirts and ties. I looked around at my fellow residents and felt out of place. They began to share about themselves, and I felt even more out of place.

Introductions began with Krishna, who had gone to Yale and Princeton and had studied physics before medical school.

The next person was Cliff. "I'm from Brown University. Both my parents are radiologists, and this is my first real job since I have grown up." Cliff had also performed in a comedy club.

Ari went next. Ari became a great friend. He shared how he had studied neuroscience in college and how he "first fell in love with the brain in college." He also said he could speak Elvish as he had taught himself the language while reading Tolkien's *The Lord of the Rings*. He had done extensive research on the brain.

Jens, my German colleague, then introduced himself. I later found out he came from a very wealthy family and had attended school at Eaton in the United Kingdom. His family even had a crest and owned a castle.

Mike from New Jersey went next. He was a very nice guy and had attended a New Jersey medical school.

Then it was my turn.

I started by saying, "Hi. I'm Chris. I did my undergrad at Idaho State University. I completed medical school at the University of Utah, and by the way, I'm married and have three children."

All of my fellow residents looked at me as if I were from another planet. Most of them said, "Idaho? Like where potatoes come from?"

"Yes," I replied, laughing. "Yes, potatoes are in Idaho."

They said, "You're married already?"

I said, "Yes, I'm married and have three children."

They were all shocked by that because most of them were not married, and having children during medical school was a very foreign notion. They gaped at me. I felt very awkward. Yet they all became some of the best friends I have ever had in my life once I really got to know them and they got to know me. They are truly some of the most wonderful people I have ever had the privilege of knowing. It was always fun for us to laugh about the first time we met, when they were talking about Ivy League schools and the amazing things they had accomplished—and then there was me: Idaho (potatoes?) graduate, married with three kids, who had somehow ended up at Johns Hopkins.

The next day was my first rotation. I was with Cliff, and we were working with Dr. Donna Magid as our attending. Cliff, who as I said had been a comedian, was very outgoing, quite talkative, and funny. As we worked, he showed his knowledge and shared everything he knew. I was more reserved in general. Growing up, I had learned to just be quiet and observe a lot. I kept my head down most of the time so as not to share anything about who I was or what I knew.

Later that day, Dr. Magid pulled me aside and said, "You need to speak up. I know you're very smart, talented, and intelligent, and you need to speak up because you have every right to be here just as they do. You've earned it, and you're just as smart as any of them. You just come from a different place and have developed a different kind of strength. You are just as talented as they are."

I really took that to heart. It really meant a lot to me that she cared enough to say that to me.

One of my other first rotations was with Elliott Fishman. When I worked with him, I got to tour the lab where he was doing his 3D imaging and 3D computer-generating techniques. Eventually, he asked me to work in his lab on some research projects. I also had the opportunity to work side by side with Karen Horton, who was a great mentor to me and many others; she worked with me to publish several articles in the medical literature.

I will always be grateful for the opportunity I had to become a part of the Johns Hopkins family. They touched my soul and will always be a part of me. If any of them read this, I wish to thank them for taking a chance on me and accepting me into their ranks. Hopkins is a special place that truly deserves the world reputation it has earned.

CHAPTER 33

Desires and Outcomes

When I close my eyes to rest, sometimes the nightmares still come in the lonely darkness, unbidden, unwelcome guests to disturb my restful sleep. But when I wake, the sun rises, and the nightmares fade into the shadows of the past as I embrace my pain. A lasting truth is that I cannot be beaten by something I don't fear. When I am able to face the past and face my fears, not hiding from them, I find a deepened resolve to vanquish them and rise triumphantly at the end of the battle.

As I share the pain and scars of my past with others, I see with greater vision the blessed life that God has given me, and I have renewed hope for the future. I have also learned to accept myself for who I am, to accept that those scars engraved on my mind and soul shaped me into who I am today. More importantly, even though I may be broken in many ways, I can love and accept myself for who I am. I no longer need to hide my past.

I spent many years running from my past, running from my scared, sad, lonely teenage self. I know now that my past is part of me. The sad, lonely teenager of my past is and always will be a part of me. Rather than hide from it, I have learned to embrace the past. By doing so, I can live my life without fear. I can be vulnerable. I can cry. I can accept myself for who I am. I can love myself and by doing so allow others to love me and love me completely. Furthermore, I believe that to love others, we need to first love ourselves.

At times we may feel broken. That is okay. Our brokenness makes us beautiful. In Japan, they have practiced the art of *kintsugi* for centuries. Kintsugi is putting broken pottery pieces back together with gold, built on the idea that by embracing flaws and imperfections rather than hiding them, you can create an even stronger, more beautiful piece of art. In much the same way, our broken selves make us beautiful and shape us into beautiful souls.

The *Christus Consolator* statue under the dome at The Johns Hopkins Hospital was one of my places of solitude during my residency. Inscribed in the base of the statue is the following verse: *Matthew 11:28-29 Come unto me, all ye that labour and are heavy laden, and I will give you rest. Take my yoke upon you, and learn of me; for I am meek and lowly in heart: and ye shall find rest unto your souls.* This message strikes me to the core as I ponder how God has truly carried me throughout my life.

I believe that at the end of our lives, we will look back and see that our lives have been a journey, a journey following a winding, barely visible path. While we are on that journey, it is hard to see the path of our lives, but if we have hope, plan, work, work, and work, we can make things better in our lives and the world. Parts of the road will be difficult, and there will be tears, tears of sadness but also tears of joy.

Sometimes it may seem easier to quit rather than continue forward. As I learned driving a dogsled, it is easier to keep moving forward than languish and sink in the snow. There will be times when we do quit or fail, and that is okay. We can rise up and try again because failure occurs only when we quit trying.

Furthermore, I know that God has a plan for us. Life might not happen the way we had planned or hoped for, but I know that if we take our broken desires, broken lives, and broken dreams; give them to God, and keep pressing forward, God's plan for our lives will unfold one word, one sentence, one page at a time and get us to the place where we should be, and that will ultimately be the best plan for us that in the beginning, we could not have even imagined. Dallin H. Oaks, a law professor and former Utah Supreme Court justice, once said, "Desires dictate our priorities, priorities shape our choices, and choices determine our actions. The desires we act on determine our changing, our achieving, and our becoming." I believe that when all is said and done, we will look back, see all the small choices we made, and see how those seemingly "insignificant" decisions have shaped our significant outcome and destination.

Despite how small and seemingly insignificant we may feel, *we all matter*, and it is up to us to make this world a better place. We just have to lean forward and leap, at times falling but trusting that after the fall we will rise, rise to heights above anything we ever imagined. For me, this was *Homeless to Hopkins* . . . just a part of my story. I have learned that as I write the story of my life, I get to wake up every day and choose. I get to write my ending. I get to choose happiness or misery, gratitude or despair. You can do the same.

CHAPTER 34

Afterword

I would like to say that we all lived happily ever after, but the truth is, our stories are still being written.

So instead, the update:

In the end, my four younger siblings and I who lived in the motels all earned doctoral degrees. One older brother also earned a doctorate. In total, six out of the ten children in my family who lived to adulthood earned doctorates, an amazing statistic in any family, even more so given the dysfunctional family in which we were raised.

Dad passed away shortly before I completed my residency. I am grateful he lived to see me become a physician. Before his passing, he obtained a patent on his device for extracting oil from oil shale. He was in the process of developing it when he died. After he passed away, I purchased a small condominium in which Mom could live so she could have some stability in her life.

All of my siblings and I have done our best to come to terms with our past and with our parents. Some have found that by remaining close; others have found peace in removing themselves in varying degrees from our mother, who still lives and still struggles. I can't speak for my siblings, but I know there will always be a degree of conflict in myself while I find the balance between forgiveness and maintaining those boundaries I have established with her. She is my mother, whom I love, and she is a daughter of God, a precious soul, who struggles. She is also a source of heartache and manipulation every time I open the door to her. Finding the balance of protecting myself yet forgiving and loving her remains my quest. With Dad's death, I find peace in seeing his wholeness and remembering his words of encouragement that gave me the courage to believe in myself. He fell short in many ways, but he always showed me love and believed in me.

After finishing my residency and fellowship at Johns Hopkins, I stayed on as faculty at the School of Medicine for some years. I have since moved to Pennsylvania and raised my five daughters there. My wife and I have found joy and satisfaction in serving in our church and in our community.

I am grateful to you, the reader, for taking your time and reading my story. Please share it with others so they may find inspiration. When your story is written, share it with others so we can all be strengthened together.

EPILOGUE

S cars. We all have them. Thank you for taking the time to let me share my scars with you. Here is a brief update to have some closure.

TEENA

Teena had nightmares for months after giving birth that she was still trapped in her body, unable to speak, see or move but only able to hear everything around her, leaving me behind to raise our children on my own. However, in time she healed, and so did her fear from the whole experience. We never thought or planned to have more children after that traumatic experience. Nevertheless, Teena would give birth to two more daughters, Aleesia and Kaitlyn, which would bring us so much joy. She has been a wonderful and supportive companion to me and a great mother to our children. She has loved helping others and has served over the past couple of decades, helping children and teen girls to feel loved and develop personal attributes that will help them throughout their lives. She has always been beside me, striving to make a difference in the lives of those around us. She is truly my best friend and the best companion one could have. I look forward to many more adventures with her.

ANGIE

We raised Angie but never officially adopted her; we were her legal guardians as designated by her parents. We raised her until she became an adult and moved out of the house. She is married with her own children now. I have always felt she was like another daughter to me. I am proud of what she has accomplished in her life.

AUTUMN

Autumn has grown up and is now married. She went to college and earned her associate's degree, and we are proud of her accomplishments. Currently, she is an executive assistant to the CEO of a rehabilitation hospital. She is happily married and has a few parakeets.

ELIANNA

EliAnna is also grown up now. She is a talented artist with a tremendous natural talent for the visual arts. I am proud of her accomplishments. Her work is on Instagram if you would like to follow her. Instagram identifier: Emiths1999.

VANESSA

I am happy to say that after several years, Teena's sister, the birth mother of Autumn and EliAnna, was able to get away from her husband, overcome her addictions, and be reunited with our family. Autumn and EliAnna are now adults and able to have a relationship with her. We have been so happy to see her overcome these obstacles in her life and finally find a place of peace and happiness. It just goes to show that there is always hope and that people can overcome insurmountable odds.

MY UPDATE

Everyone has experiences in life that result in what I call *demons*. They are the shadows and aftereffects of overcoming the trials and hardships of life. We can't see them, we don't like to talk about them, we don't like to face them, and I don't know that they ever really go away. I want to say that hard work and God got me through, that I lived happily ever after, with few hellhounds to haunt my adult life. The truth is, God and hard work *did* get me through life and help me to move forward *despite* my demons, spawned decades ago in a childhood defined by chaos and uncertainty.

I have not come this far unscathed; my demons include mistrust, anxiety, and PTSD. I was taught from an early age not to trust anyone, as they would try to use or manipulate me. I was raised more in fear than love. Thus, fear, not love, is the first emotion I remember from my childhood, and it is the one that defined it. Fear nourished my anxiety, and delayed stress symptoms eventually surfaced as a result of both.

During a tough time in my adult life, when my past was haunting me, my wife came to me and quoted Viktor Frankl: "In some ways suffering ceases to be suffering at the moment it finds a meaning, such as the meaning of a sacrifice."

She then suggested that if I could take all those things that I went through and use them to help others, perhaps my suffering would find its meaning and free me from such suffering.

That was the beginning of my quest to open up and share what I have been through in the hope of helping others. It was also the beginning of the lengthy process of writing this memoir. Because I was taught to distrust others, I had developed protective walls to reduce my vulnerability. It took me decades to even begin to tear down those walls and share these events with others. In fact, I did not completely open up to my wife about my disordered childhood experiences until we had been married for many years.

The process of writing this book has been quite therapeutic in that I have worked through those events, finally starting to accept them for what they were. I have shed many tears writing this memoir, but they have allowed me to show my authentic self. But, of course, all is not idyllic, nor should I expect it to be.

In addition to the occasional anxiety and PTSD, specific triggers lead me to feel panic. I still overthink everything and make backup plans—and a backup to my backup plans—and stand ever ready for action should my world start to fall apart again.

Yet fear no longer consumes me, and love has replaced it. I have finally learned how to love and trust by finding love and trust in others, and, more importantly, I have learned to love and trust myself and God.

I worked at letting myself be vulnerable. I went to therapy for several years to accept those past events in my life. Therapy was beneficial, as it helped me to open up and let the world see the true me.

I will always have scars, but now I can wear them for what they have become: reminders of the battles I have fought and the victories I have attained through the Grace of God.

I now find peace in sharing my trials and successes with others. I am actively involved in programs to support people who are homeless. I am a member of the National Coalition for Homelessness, and I speak at fundraising events to raise money for programs to combat homelessness.

I know now that it is okay not to be okay, and it is okay to struggle even after achieving success. When you have lived in a situation where your basic needs are unmet, even though you may have created a new life of abundance, that "hunger" never goes away.

One of my heroes, Dwayne Johnson, stated how I feel quite well: "I'll never, ever be full. I'll always be hungry. Obviously, I'm not talking about food. Growing up, I had nothing for such a long time. Someone told me a long time ago, and I've never forgotten it, 'Once you've ever been hungry, really, really hungry, then you'll never, ever be full.'"

I have used that drive to become the hardest working person in the room. It has been a strength for me, but it is also a curse. Because of the hunger that is a part of my soul, I often work more than I should. I spread myself too thin. Similar to when I was in school, work is now my safe space. When I am working, I focus entirely, and all my baggage disappears for that moment. I excel at my job just as I did in school. It is when I have downtime that my anxiety surfaces. But, at the end of the day, I can look back and be satisfied that I am blessed to have felt the hand of God in my life.

Without His assistance, I could not have achieved anything in my life. This fact is the most important thing I need to acknowledge in my path from homeless to Hopkins: the hand of God has been in my life. His Grace and divine influence opened the impossible pathways of my life. When I was young, I never imagined that I would become a physician, not to mention the near-zero probability that I would have the privilege to be at a special place like Johns Hopkins. I know that I did not accomplish these accolades merely through my own efforts; it was His direct involvement in my life that gave me my strength, and the credit should be given to Him. We are all children of God, irrespective of religion, race, country, or gender, whether we are rich or poor, old or young. He loves all of us and wants us to have our best life. We all are important to Him, as we are His children. If we turn to Him and give Him our scars and demons, He can heal us; we only need to ask.

We do not need to carry the baggage of the past with us. We can give the past back to God and let Him take that weight. When we carry the weight of the past alone, we become mired. We don't move forward; we are filled with sadness, rage, distrust, and despair. Like my experience with the dog sled, we slide along on top of the snow as we continue moving forward. When we stop, we become stuck in the snow, unable to move forward without great effort. If we remove the baggage from the sled, our sled is lightened, and we can again move forward. When we move forward, leaving that baggage with God, the tracks of the past follow us in the snow, but they don't define our future. We can choose our future path, choose our future joy, and choose our future happiness.

It does not matter where you start. It does not matter what profession you choose or what educational level you have obtained. Few people who read this may become a physician or be privileged to attend an elite institution. Life is not a competition to earn the most titles, honors, or money; at the end of life, those things won't matter. Rather, life is a journey to choose to live a fulfilling and happy life; to choose and find your own path, your own happiness.

I know that I have value and worth, even though I am scarred. Are we not all scarred in one way or another? Our scars should unite us rather than divide us. That is what makes us beautiful. It makes us real. It makes us human.

It means we have lived a life.